Not Every Bank is Goldman Sachs

Tracking the rise of algorithmic machines and high frequency trading through a deregulated investment world

Book 4 of The Complete Banker series

By Chris Skinner

The
**Complete
Banker**

First published 2010 by Balatro Limited, 98 Westbury Lane, Buckhursthill, IG9 5PW, UK

ISBN 978-1-907720-09-3

Edited and produced by Searching Finance Ltd, 8 Whitehall Road, London W7 2JE, UK. Tel: +44 (0) 7885 441682; email: enquiries@searchingfinance.co.uk; web: www.searchingfinance.co.uk

Editor: Ann Tierney

Typeset by: Deirdré Gyenes

Not Every Bank is Goldman Sachs

Tracking the rise of algorithmic machines and high frequency trading through a deregulated investment world

Book 4 of The Complete Banker series

By Chris Skinner

The
**Complete
Banker**

About Chris Skinner

Chris has been providing independent, expert commentary on the key developments in banking for over a decade in his role as Chief Executive of Balatro and Chairman of the Financial Services Club. In particular, he has been writing for various media, such as the Banker Magazine, since 2004 and is a key commentator on banking for prime time news channels including the BBC, Sky and Bloomberg. Prior to creating his independent entities, Chris had key roles at management and board levels covering insurance, retail and investment banking across a range of consulting and technology firms.

Chris Skinner has worked worldwide delivering advice, keynote speeches, presentations and workshops to many banks and vendors worldwide, including Accenture, American Express, ANZ, Bank of America, Bank of Baroda, Cisco, Hewlett Packard, Liberty Bank, Lloyds TSB, McKinsey, Merrill Lynch, Microsoft, National Australia Bank, Nationwide Building Society, NCR, TATA, the National Bank of Kuwait, the Union Bank of the Philippines, Wachovia Bank, Washington Mutual, and many others.

About the Financial Services Club

The Financial Services Club is a unique service aimed at senior executives and decision makers from banks, insurance companies, technology firms, consultancies ... in fact, any firm that is interested in understanding and planning for the future operating environment for the financial services markets.

The Financial Services Club bridges the gap between today and tomorrow. It allows you to network with hundreds of professionals all sharing a common interest in the future of the industry. The Club hosts over 50 events a year, in a number of different European countries, with keynote speakers and luminaries from the industry airing their views on the future of financial services. Our illustrious speaker list is targeted to cover all aspects of the industry from practitioners to legislators to futurists.

For more information, go to http://www.fsclub.co.uk

Contents

Chapter 4 The trading infrastructure: latency, light speed and dark pools

Chapter 5 New trading venues and incumbent exchanges

Chapter 6 Clearing and settlement

Preface

What to call a book about investment banking, capital markets, algorithmic high frequency trading, the Markets in Financial Instruments Directive (MiFID) – the EU Directive that has radically changed these markets – and more? That's a challenge, and so I thought about calling it 'A Guide to Capital Markets' or something equally dull, and then realised that it had to be 'Not every bank is Goldman Sachs'.

Why?

Because Goldman Sachs is easily the most controversial of all the banks in the world today. They are likened to a giant "vampire squid", sucking the life and money out of everything through their tentacles reaching worldwide. They are accused of causing every stock market crash and disaster throughout history. They pay bonuses that are obscene by the general standards of you and me, and they seem to have zero tolerance for anyone but themselves.

These are the big swinging dicks, masters of the universe, the Gordon Geckos of the 21st century.

Another view is that they are doing "God's work", creating liquidity and trading in goods and services that otherwise could not be traded. They are bringing innovation to global stock markets, and enabling alpha returns to their investors that are far in excess of what could be achieved with any other bank. They are the bank that sets the leadership that all others follow, and are to be admired and revered.

Whichever your view, the undeniable truth is that Goldman Sachs is the one investment bank to ride through the crisis at the end of the 2000s in style and intact. Unlike their brethren at Bear Stearns, Merrill Lynch and Lehman Brothers, Goldman Sachs, along with Morgan Stanley, are still independent and still going strong. A few others have replaced their old competition, particularly Nomura and Barclays Capital, and a few others are still on the horizon, and the markets are made by these few.

Serving these market makers are new platforms and exchanges that have taken the mantle from the old exchanges. You may think that London Stock Exchange, Deutsche Bourse, the New York Stock Exchange and NASDAQ are the big trading names for example, but that is changing. Chi-X and BATS are new usurpers of those old dominant names, as are the Shanghai and Mumbai Stock Exchanges, so the world is different.

How is the investment world changing and what are the key trends to track?

This book reviews all of these areas and more, including the regulatory landscape, MiFID, the challenges with clearing and settlement, and more.

So, if you want to understand capital markets and investment banking and just why they get those big bonuses, this is a short guide for you.

Meantime, if you want to become a complete banker, then keep adding our small works of observations about the industry to your knowledge by buying some of the other books about banking in the Complete Banker series.

Have fun and enjoy the read,

Chris

PS: The articles herein have been selected from white papers, presentations and other research I have undertaken, and from my regular Financial Services Club blog postings; at http://www.thefinanser.com; for more information on the Financial Services Club, go to http://www.fsclub.co.uk

Chapter 1 The future for investment and trading

Introduction

In the mid-2000s, I was regularly told the joke that the City/Wall Street would soon be run by one man and his dog. The man is there to feed the dog. The dog is there to stop the man touching the computers. A scary image of the future, or realistic? Certainly, it's not that far off the truth, with over half of the major trading markets of the world now running on completely automated servers. So let's look at what's happening out there and see what the future might be a few more years downstream.

How far can investment firms innovate? (2010)

I'm continually impressed and amazed by the speed of change in the technology of the investment markets.

For example, last year was all talk about low latency and lit versus dark pools. This year, it's all about private cloud-based services based upon co-location and proximity services. Next year, it will be all about real-time liquidity and settlement.

Equally, the change from old to new trading venues is quite surprising. I was chatting with one of the MTFs yesterday for example. An MTF is a Multilateral Trading Facility, a new class of exchange introduced by MiFID, the Markets in Financial Instruments Directive. The conversation reminded me that only two years ago, everyone was saying that liquidity doesn't move and there would be no threat to traditional exchanges from these new trading venues.

Two years later, Chi-X has more trading and market share than the London Stock Exchange (LSE); LSE has acquired Turquoise and completely changed strategy and direction; Euronext has launched a major dark pool; Deutsche Bourse is heavily expanding in ultra low latency connections, targeting latencies under 3.3 milliseconds for Frankfurt-Amsterdam, under 4.5 milliseconds for Frankfurt-Paris, under 40 milliseconds for Frankfurt-New York, and under 49 milliseconds for Frankfurt-Chicago ...

... and so it goes on.

Just two years ago, many exchanges thought that seconds were fine. Today it's milliseconds. Tomorrow it's microseconds. And then what?

Is it to achieve the ever elusive cross-asset class trading system? The one where a paired equities trade can be combined with an FX hedge across a global arbitrage?

Nah, we've already got that.

Is it to innovate new instruments, even when the last set of instruments – Structured Investment Vehicles, Credit Default Swaps and Collateralised Debt Orders – screwed up the world's economies? Nah, we've already got that too.

Is it to bring on board new exchanges and focus on emerging markets? Nah, we've already got emerging markets, cross-asset class structure exchange products.

So what is the next wave of major change in trading systems and markets, and how will governments manage to derisk the next wave of innovation?

Well, if the move does become one where real-time execution is combined with real-time settlement and real-time risk management, then the challenge for broker-dealers will be to bring added value to clients through arbitraging across venues and instruments. But hey, that's what they do now, isn't it?

Of course. It's what broker-dealers and market-markers have done for all time and will be what they do for the future.

You see, the challenge is to keep up with the innovations of a Goldman Sachs and it is the reason why Goldmans made $100 million profits for every day of trading last year. Now there's a fine line between making markets and moving markets, and that's the line Goldman walk. It will be interesting to see how Goldman and company make markets in the future, between the Obama tax and the new regulatory regime. But the key will be to continue to innovate with technology ... and they are and will be.

That is why we are moving towards an almost seamless order flow through execution through settlement system, thanks to smart order routing combined with execution management systems. That's one of this year's big buzzes in trading tech, especially as Asia has followed Europe and America's approach with Japan clearing the way for new Alternative Trading Systems and venues.

So perhaps the big buzz will really be about arbitraging across venues and instruments using global smart order routing, combined with real-time execution and settlement in microseconds.

Hmmm ... sounds risky to me.

Will governments be up to the job of regulating all of these new innovations?

Capital markets statistics (2010)

According to a report from TheCity UK:

- Companies raised £83 billion on the London Stock Exchange in 2009, including £5 billion raised on AIM, the market designed specifically for smaller, high growth companies.
- An additional £21 million was raised on PLUS, which also caters for smaller high growth companies.
- Of the 1,038 UK companies quoted on AIM, 603 are based outside London, as are 42 per cent of the companies on PLUS.

Meanwhile, FX transactions have gone through the roof, ever since they became a tradable instrument on the foreign exchange markets. This BIS chart of the Global FX transactions since 1992 shows the impact this has had:

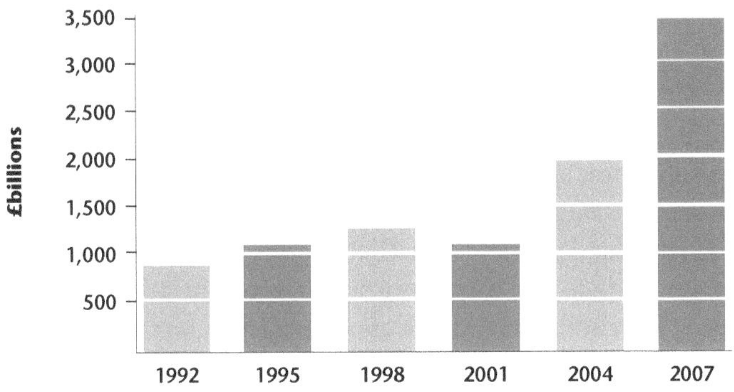

Source: Bank for International Settlement

Of course, this has to be combined with globalisation, so here's the world's trade volume growth from 2000 through 2009:

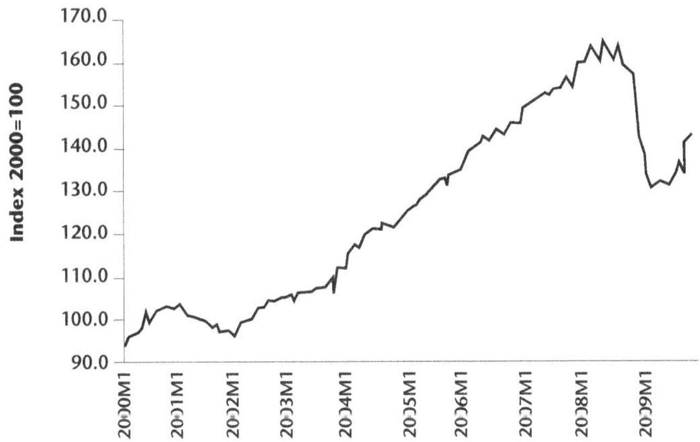

Source: World Trade Monitor, CPB Netherlands Bureau for Economic Policy Analysis, October 2009

Charts sourced from TheCity UK report

One large, connected server farm (2009)

Like most good conferences, the Deutsche Bourse Open Day had sponsors. These sponsors are generally partners with the exchange however, working with them to deliver technology solutions. The four highlighted partners were Colt, Corvil, Equinix and Orc.

Each of them had a moment in the spotlight as sponsor, to present their solution and talk about what they were up to, so I sat in that stream through the day to get a feel of the latest and greatest in trading technologies. And it was interesting.

As mentioned already, the main topic was speed. The speed of connectivity via proximity hosting solutions and co-location. Colt focused upon the former and Equinix on the latter, and both were detailing how this improves a broker's speeds and feeds.

In Colt's case, we are looking at speeds of sub-400 milliseconds for a round the world trip for a trade instruction. In Equinix's, the focal point is having everything sitting in one data centre for high speed connectivity.

They enthral the listener with stories of Chicago to Frankfurt communications in 50 milliseconds, or data centres that offer 1.2 million square feet of server capability. The latter came from Equinix who apparently have 43 data centres in 10 countries, with 1.2 million square feet of server capacity in the USA.

1.2 million square feet of co-location space. 1.2 million square feet. That's over 20 football fields'-worth of computer power. And that's just in the US of A, as they boast a further 10 football fields worth (600,000 square feet) in Asia and Europe.

That's racks upon racks upon grids upon grids upon boards upon motherboards of compute capacity. Just unbelievable.

It's also where I get this idea of a future being one where all the exchanges, market-makers and broker-dealers of the world just co-locate themselves in a few massive data centres around the world connected by low latency dark fibre.

Just unbelievable.

Meanwhile, Corvil talked about the idea of low latency being all well and good but, when you have hand-offs between the trader, the exchange and the price feeds, it all falls apart.

Their game is all about managing latency between the links and put up a nice little formula of how to calculate latency:

Latency = PD + SD + QD

- PD being the Propagation Delay of speeds and feeds and distance;
- SD being the Serialisation Delay of message sizes and bandwidth; and
- QD being the Queuing Delay of message arrivals and scheduling

All and each of these factors have an impact, and even with co-location and proximity hosting, you still get delays in the system between each point end-to-end.

I particularly liked their picture of real-life trading environments, which shows how 1 microsecond can make such a difference. In a microsecond you can make or break a trade execution. In a microsecond you can win the arbitrage game or lose it. In a microsecond, you can get the spread, buck the market and secure the deal.

And in the time it's taken you to read this, about 100 million deals have been secured. Blink and you'll miss them.

Oh yes, why write about some of the firms out there supplying the markets? Because I found it interesting that Deutsche Bourse had selected these firms as partners and sponsors.

I wonder who the other exchanges would put on stage?

The future vision for trading (2009)

At a Deutsche Bourse Open Day for IT, I chaired a panel comprising senior figures from Eurex, the International Securities Exchange and IBM. The focus of the panel was the future of trading technologies, and was a wide ranging discussion covering everything, from dark pools to high frequency trading (HFT).

Questions abounded, such as:

Q: Is HFT good or bad for liquidity, as it gives large players an unfair advantage over small to mid size players and allows market abuses such as flash orders and front running?

A: As long as everyone has equal access to the markets, then it is no issue. The fact that some traders cannot afford the technologies to deal in flash orders is not an unequal market perspective; it's just that some are better at doing this and can afford the systems to do it. There is no barrier to entry however.

(BTW, I totally disagree with that view)

Q: At these speeds, is it technically impossible to do compliance? For example, Barclays Capital is just one illustration of the markets becoming more difficult to manage when they are fined for not even being able to get the timing right on a trade execution.

A: Yes, this is more difficult but time stamping trades is an essential core competence of any trading house. The issue lies with low latency and how a broker deals with order flow. If you cannot time stamp effectively when an order is received, filled and executed throughout the trade flow then you are not delivering on that core competence.

This happened recently with TD Securities, which was accused of front running trades, and yet how do you prove you weren't front running when everything takes place in a microsecond? TD Securities fought off a recent investigation to prove they were not front running by being able to demonstrate timings through their order flow, and so yes, keeping time is a basic requirement today.

Q: What about the whole aspect of the changing regulatory regime with the new rules being developed by the G20, the de Larosiere report, the confirmation that there will be a MiFID 2, etc. In fact, MiFID 2, according to a speech by Charlie McCreevy in Dublin recently, will incorporate OTC derivatives in its next iteration. What does all of this mean for trade execution and technologies?

A: The markets are ready for more regulation although it is interesting that most regulation creates unintended consequences. For example, the law of intended consequences is demonstrated by MiFID where the aim of the regulation was to have more transparency and openness and what did we get? More opaqueness, price fragmentation and a growing off-exchange trading environment using technology to create dark pools. This is the key to the technology used in the trading environment- to create arbitrage, risk and profitability for the client.

Meanwhile, everything will move towards real-time reporting. For example, Eurex is already able to provide real-time clearing at trade execution. Firms will move towards this model for real-time trade reporting and real-time risk and liquidity management.

Q: What about social media & Twitter? Don't these tools support insider trading? Do we end up with all traders being searched for personal communication devices before they enter the trade floor?

A: No, you don't need to go to that extent. Facebook and Twitter are electronic communication tools however, so they need to be brought under the controls and disciplines of compliance regulations or be blocked and, if a trader is found in contravention of such in-house policies, then it's a disciplinary dressing-down and possibly termination of employment. But you can do things about these areas. For example, research into this area clearly shows that the US regulatory rules apply just as much to tweets as they do to email. And there are tools you can implement to monitor such activities and store and forward such information, which is the right approach to take.

Q: How do you see the development of cloud computing in the trading markets?

A: In the US, we have seven major exchanges and I can see the world developing into one where those seven exchanges all place their servers in a massive server farm, co-located with market makers and brokers, so that the systems can deal in real-time. That's where we are almost at today and certainly will be moving in that direction more and more over time.

(The answers above were my own take on the discussions, by the way, rather than quotes from the panellists, but you get the idea of the flow.)

We finished with a vision of the future of trading which I will sum up as being a world where each continent has a massive data centre of co-located servers representing the main trading venues of each economy.

The European data centres will naturally locate in London, Paris and Frankfurt; America's will be in New York, Chicago and possibly San Francisco; Latin America's in San Paolo and Buenos Aires; Asia's in Mumbai, Tokyo, Shanghai, Hong Kong and Australia; and Africa and the Middle East will be based in Johannesburg and Dubai (or Bahrain or Qatar dependent upon how the region's financial centres compete for dominance).

Fourteen massive data centres with mirroring and backup for each other. Effectively, a massive cloud of trade execution.

And yes, that's where we move towards – a secure global cloud computing environment, all linked by dark fibre between 14 massive data centres. The data centres house the world's exchanges and their broker dealers. They can transact in microseconds within exchange and, thanks to terabit lines, can send a trade execution around the world in under a millisecond.

Lightning dealings in order flows through smart order systems that allow billions of offers and bids to be matched in a millisecond.

All of this liquidity flow being watched under a traffic light system of liquidity risk and market monitoring, such that market abuses are visualised and captured during the trade flow in real-time.

The G20 agreements on co-located data centre environments dealt with that one after the financial crisis of 2013, when the dark fibre smart order routers allowed Goldman Sachs to front run ...

Aw shucks, now I'm just getting cynical again aren't I?

The Future Trader (2008)

The Future Trader has:

- Unlimited bandwidth and storage allows complete market access, storage and knowledge;
- Super-intelligent algo and multi-asset trading direct from the home, with smart order routing intelligence built into the network;
- Highly complex cross-asset class trading strategies delivered direct to the execution venues with no 'sell-side' broker-dealer involved – just trading and execution;
- Broker-dealers now compete as execution venues with traditional exchanges whilst others have evolved to be specialist research analytics houses or boutique advisors;
- Interactions with systems are intuitive and intelligent with voice and video interfaces, rather than mouse and keyboard;
- Collaborative work with colleagues is through hi-definition video wall conferencing from home, rather than through 100-storey office blocks in downtown city venues.

Scenario: Lee Nixon, Future Trader, water commodities

Lee Nixon opened his eyes as the room's walls illuminated to intensity level 4. The walls were set to brighten gradually from 1:45 a.m. and it was now 2:00. Another 15 minutes and intensity level 10 would have been like a bright summer's day.

Lee liked the luminescent orange sunrise effect of the walls best as it made him feel warm and summery, even though the world outside was deep in the snows of winter and the dark of night. He usually woke at this time though, as he was known as a leader in futures trading in the world's rarest commodity: water.

Water had been recognised as a potentially lucrative commodity market since the late 1990s, when the International Water Management Institute[1] estimated that Earth would need 17% more water by 2025 than the water resources available at that time, in order to feed the world. The trouble was that no-one in the investment markets or elsewhere could really see how to capitalise on this opportunity until the 2011 Mercury Bomb when terrorists poured liquid mercury into Lake Meade, the largest reservoir in the USA. It was enough to wipe out all water supplies from the Lake for six months, and created a massive water shortage which cost the US Federal Reserve $35 billion to overcome.

This single incident led to water becoming the world's hottest commodity, thanks to the US government's introduction of the Water Act in 2012. This Act allowed Water firms to not only trade as organisations, but also to trade their future water supplies based upon each of their water purification plants, reservoirs and facilities. The higher the government approved rating the water facility, the greater the liquidity of the stock in that utility.

Now that the world's equities and future markets had broken into highly automated trading facilities, where not only fractions of stocks could be traded but also fractions of firms, the introduction of the Water Act and the consequent knock-on effect in other jurisdictions, had led to an explosion of trading in water.

Exotic water options trading on the Water Commodities Exchange (WCE) based in London became one of the most liquid markets, literally, and Lee was known as the world's leading water options trader. Having said that, Lee lives in Boston which is why he was getting up at 2:00 in the morning. Not because he wanted to catch the opening of the markets as he would have done in the old days – there is no opening or closing of markets, markets trade 24 hours – but because he wanted to catch WaterWorld, the daily news update on the world's water resources broadcast in London from 8:00 to 8:30 on Water.net, the new dedicated Water Channel.

Of course, he could preset to catch WaterWorld and view it later on his watch or in his PTV, but then he would miss the opportunity to catch the trading liquidity during the first half-hour after the programme's ending. Everyone watched WaterWorld if they were involved in the water commodities markets.

Lee began his day as usual with a fast all-round shower and air-dry whilst dealing with any urgent messages. The shower panels, doors, walls ... everything was built for connection in his purpose-built pod. Therefore, whilst showering, Lee was bringing up video screens in his Perspex-style shower screen simply by moving his hands around the screen to move different messages to where he wanted to see them or save them. As a result, he could check his messages easily whilst washing, with each message appearing in a specific space based upon where Lee pointed.

First, there were a few video messages from other traders around the world, then a viewcard from his girlfriend who was travelling Asia and a commentary from his mother asking why he never viewed her. No change there.

After air-drying and pouring himself some detox juice, the next part of the daily routine was to watch the market movements using Market Recorder.

Market Recorder is a service provided by his employer, Slate Street, and is designed to be used by all of their traders globally. It does what it says on the tin: records the markets. All market data, brokers, prices, exchanges, execution venues, liquidity pools ... everything globally is recorded by Market Recorder.

The great thing is that each trader can then build dynamic trading strategies and test them through Market Recorder by fine-tuning dealings they may have made over the last few hours, days, months and years.

Each trader would also use Market Recorder in a different way. For example, if you were dealing in energy futures then you would use Market Recorder to record the main execution venues for the energy desk, which typically came down to Enex: the merged Nymex and ICE exchange.

But water was far more important than oil or gas, and Lee used Market Recorder to record the WCE (the Water Commodities Exchange) as that was the only venue that counted for him, although he did use eBanyse, the eBay managed NYSE, as well, because it was ideal for generic equity dealings in the world's water firms through a single low latency global connection.

The fact is that the unlimited storage and indexing facilities offered by Market Recorder meant that it could record all of these market movements across all of these trading venues. Not only that but it could retain market tick data and associated feeds for twelve months in real-time and for five years in near-time. That way any trader could review their dealings against the market movements for as far back as most of them ever wanted, on any market venue, for any stock, bond or commodity in the world.

In order to use Market Recorder, Lee began by asking the service to playback yesterday's markets, his dealings, trades executed and rejected, returns through the day and so forth. This sounds simple but is much more complex in practice.

For example, the first thing Market Recorder does is present Lee with screens on the video wall. The video wall he's using at this point is around six feet tall by nine feet wide, and there are six screens running.

The first screen linked to the WCE as well as his other primary water execution venues of interest such as eBanyse, the next showed his total water portfolio, a third showed his position by each broker and venue, another showed his position against the other Slate Street water traders – he wasn't the only one, but was recognised as the leader of the Water Desk, a fifth showed his position of trading and return against each market over the past 12 months and a sixth showed projected water supplies, firms and purification plants news and forecasts released during the same period.

Lee assimilated all of this information in seconds – he was used to it – and then began to ask for simulations of actions he might have take the previous day. Market Recorder not only played out his positions, but showed recommendations as to where he could have improved his position and portfolio, as well as marking his positive movements. The service allowed him to very quickly roll forward and roll back against positions to see how things would have worked out if he had made those decisions.

One of the biggest changes over the decade before is that all of his interactions with Market Recorder were being delivered through voice commands and hand movements – the keyboard had died out in the early 2010s as visual and touch communications became pervasive – and he was trying various ideas out before the WaterWorld broadcast to see how he could have improved his returns on the previous day.

The other big change in Lee's approach, compared to the way markets operated ten years before, is that he had no primary broker or sell-side firms to deal with. For a while, brokers had pushed technology heavily towards the buy-side with Execution Management Systems integrated with Order Management Systems, along with highly complex algo trading tools.

Lee's world was different, as all of these tools were built into Market Recorder which incorporated incredible smart routing intelligence. The result is that Lee did not even think about which firm or firms to trade through and did not check who executed which trades the day before. All trades were handled by Market Recorder itself, which basically would look at what Lee was trying to achieve and how, and then would route his requirements intelligently to any execution venue globally that could take the order based upon his requirements for speed, latency, price and cost.

That is why, although WCE was his main choice of trading venue for water commodities, it did not mean Lee traded there ... instead, he used the WCE to give him the best knowledge of what was happening in the water markets. That is why Lee's orders in play at 2:00 in Boston were actually being routed direct to Hong Kong. But he had no interest in such mundane trivia, as the Market Recorder handled all of that for him.

Information was Lee's top priority. Information to guide him in his investment process and strategy, and that is why Lee enjoyed the flexibility of the six-screen system which he could supplement with live news and other video services to enrich his knowledge base.

After half an hour of getting up to speed with the markets, WaterWorld came onto the Water Channel so he stopped playing with his portfolio and watched the feed coming in live. He also connected now with the other Slate Street water traders around the globe, with Yin in Kuala Lumpur, Dave in London, Theresa in Sydney and Sean in San Francisco.

The traders had no need to be based in the centres of water markets as information was their lifeblood. Having said that, they would all meet online at least once a day to trade knowledge on a viewcall. Those meetings were always planned for three hours after WaterWorld but, during WaterWorld, they would talk using their video wall.

So, Lee now had a video wall next to his breakfast workout table that looked a little like a weird chess board, with six small screens from Market Recorder running in the lower portion of the wall, four 17" widescreen views of Yin, Dave, Theresa and Sean running across the top of the wall, and a large 60" screen of WaterWorld in the centre.

During the broadcast each of them made commentary. Their words were automatically being translated into subtitles by the intelligent voice recognition systems built into their systems. These subtitles appeared on-screen against each of their views.

Yin was commenting on China's Three Gorges Dam, run by Aqua America, and the fact the Government had ordered that the ageing processing plant needed to be upgraded by 2020, whilst Dave was sharing news that Russia's Gazprom had just made a bid to add the German utility RWE, which owned various water firms including the UK's Thames Water, to their portfolio. This would make Gazprom the world's largest integrated water and energy firm, and a further possible stranglehold on the markets.

Meantime, the Water Channel's WaterWorld broadcast was focusing on the breaking news of floods in California due to a mini-tsunami in San Diego. All eyes turned to Sean who was already on the case and reassured them that this had been forecast for 10:12 p.m. PST, but the fact it had hit at 10:14 would not cause an issue in their dealings.

As WaterWorld ended, they all returned to Market Recorder whilst leaving their video screens running. This was the way the 'team' worked – as a virtual team, all in touch via their video wall. Each could switch position to the other's Market Recorder view in real-time if required – in order to see the trading strategies of others in the network – or they could bring up a summary screen showing their position against the other Slate Street water traders as part of their main interface.

Lee programmed his trading, which included buying 1,000 shares short on Gazprom with an offset hedge of long on RWE in case the merger discussions failed, laying off Aqua America shares bundled with an increase in position in China's largest water processing utility, Sinowater. As part of his portfolio, Market Recorder recommended that he add a Yuan option as part of the Sinowater investment, as well as placing a bold hedge on water yields in the US markets post the tsunami and based upon the strength of the hit taken in San Diego.

This continued as a real-time dialogue with Market Recorder through the rest of day until 6:00 EST when, as per usual, the viewcalls for the day began.

Viewcalls delivered high quality communications that allowed the Water Desk team to come together as a virtual team each day. Effectively, if gave Lee a six foot tall by nine foot wide view of the other four guys in his group. Even though they were all spread around the world, they could just as easily have been there in the room with him, as the hi-definition three-dimensional connection felt real.

That is why no-one needed to meet or trade in an office block, but had the beauty of global, 24*7 trading facilitated from each of their personal pod spaces.

The future of the City of London (2009)

I've seen a couple of bits of commentary in the past week about the City of London losing its strength, namely: 'City's dominance in doubt' (The *Telegraph*), and 'London ponders its future as financial powerhouse' (*New York Times*).

During the boom years of the 2000s, London competed with Frankfurt and New York to become the financial centre of the world – and won. Michael Bloomberg hired McKinsey to see what was happening to Wall Street in 2006 and their subsequent report admitted defeat to London's financial strengths. Frankfurt meantime stuttered and coughed on London's sheer dominance.

The question these articles raise is whether the City's strength can continue, or is it a busted flush as a result of the financial crisis?

To answer such a question we have to go back to the deregulation of the City back in the 1980s under Margaret Thatcher, the so-called 'Big Bang'.

Following the dramatic changes of October 1987, when the City was dramatically restructured into an electronic trading playground, London has been one of the most open and transparent markets in which to partake in financial activities anywhere in the world.

The result has been a massive rise in employment in our financial markets and related expertise, with 420,000 people working in financial services in the City and Canary Wharf, and a further 300,000 people in related services from technology through legal to hospitality services.

Such success has been a major driver of the UK economy, with financial services contributing a major slice of the UK's GDP. For example, at the peak of the industry's growth in 2007, British banks represented over 1 million jobs; £70bn of the UK's national output or 6.8 per cent of GDP; and 25 per cent of the country's total corporation tax (£8bn).

Then Northern Rock imploded, soon to be followed by the major market meltdown of September 2008 that resulted from Lehman Brothers collapse, itself caused by its exposure to the credit default swaps market that had reached $62 trillion in 2007 from a mere $1 trillion in 2001. It was this market's failure that caused the world to pump $5 trillion into the system to try to revive the global financial sector.

Many say that this is now resulting in a change of outlook and the end of capitalism. If that's the case, is London's hey-day gone? The answer is: 'of course not'. Just because banks and bankers have a bad name right now does not mean that all banks and bankers are bad. The rotten apples are a small number compared to the hundreds of thousands who work in the City and the high level of skills they contribute.

A decade ago, when LIFFE failed to compete with Eurex and Frankfurt dominated the European derivatives and futures markets, it was believed that London was a busted flush but now more people work in the City than populate Frankfurt. London's competitive advantages are clear: location, skills, knowledge, expertise and access. Nowhere else in Europe has such density of capability and London also is the centre of an English-speaking country that forms the bridgehead for an English-speaking world. The density of our knowledge base and the degree of openness have been a critical differentiation for the City in our past, and will be in our future.

Though London's light-touch, principles-based self-regulating approach, which made it the 'easy-to-do-business-with' centre of the trading world, is now broken, that system is broken across the world. And the fact that the FSA failed in its duties, and the triumvirate approach of the FSA, Treasury and Bank of England failed, is not a matter unique to the UK. The SEC failed in America, as did their triumvirate of the SEC, Treasury and Federal Reserve.

Equally, you could point to failings in the European Central Bank and their associated authorities. This still does not take away, reduce or substitute the City's unique features of skills, knowledge, expertise and access, all in one location in an English-speaking hub.

The City's reputation has been damaged but it is not a mortal wound, just a scar left by a joyride led by Wall Street which London pursued blindly in order to keep up. Henceforth, common sense must dictate that if you see a joyride, don't get on it; if you see a bandwagon, don't get on it; if you are on a rollercoaster, try and get off. The fact is that the financial markets move in a herd mentality and if you irrationally join that herd because everyone's making money, then you know something's wrong.

That's why so many seasoned investors looked at the internet boom of the 1990s and said it wouldn't last, and it didn't. Warren Buffet referred to complex derivatives as 'weapons of financial destruction' back in 2002 and so they proved to be. And that's why everyone said the housing market boom and consumer-based demand-led economies of Britain and the US were unsustainable, and they were. They were just fuelled by the irrational exuberance of a flawed risk model for credit default swaps in the shadow financial markets and leverage.

What is the future for the City of London's financial marketplace? Answer: about the same but with two big changes.

The first change is that the Bank of England is gaining much greater powers through the Banking Act of 2009 and can now ask tough questions of those operating in the UK. The Bank will need to focus very heavily on looking for unsubstantiated profits and growth in the financial markets. The unchecked irrational exuberance of a bubble blowing must be caught early by checking to see whether there is actually any underlying collateral creating the bubble or whether it is all just air.

The unchecked exuberance of both the internet and credit bubbles were obvious; it is just that no-one asked the tough questions of where the collateral was to fuel such booms. The Bank must be the one to ask those questions in the future and then be even braver: to pull out of the boom before it bursts.

The hardest part about living in a boom is to turn your back on it and, even worse, to have to tell those national institutions involved in such hedonism to give it up.

But the Bank's role in the future must be to actively seek out such hedonism and burst it, control it and keep it in check. The official national party-pooper, in other words.

The second big change is that the City must no longer look to the US for its leadership, but must actively become neutral in its standing in the world. Every country and nation should be treated as an equal player on the City's stage, subject to that country's credit, ethical and moral ratings. The City must be as easy-to-do-business-with for the Chinese and Indians as the Americans and Europeans. The City should actively engage in building infrastructure and capability to trade as a preferred destination for developed economies as well as those that are emerging, subject to those countries' credit, ethics and moral issues.

The City has a strong future as an open trading centre for the world's financial markets as long as the supervisory bodies have the guts and the teeth to regulate effectively and the institutions have the appetite and the ability to embrace all economies on a neutral basis.

Given those caveats, I believe the City of London will be thriving and successful for many years to come.

Chapter 2 The impact of MiFID and other regulations

Introduction

I spend a lot of time looking at regulations in capital markets, with the two major laws of the last few years being the Markets in Financial Instruments Directive (MiFID) in Europe and RegNMS in the USA. These are now being supplemented by new laws post the financial crisis, such as the 2010 Dodd-Frank regulations in the USA that lock down and limit proprietary trading by banks on their own books. Equally, MiFID is being updated and revised through the next few years, so we'll keep coming back to these areas as new laws are the best way to create new innovation, new banks and new ways of working.

Is MiFID working? (2010)

Just had an enjoyable morning floating around the City and talking with folks about MiFID 2. Now you may think that's not so enjoyable, but it has been interesting.

For a while now, MiFID (Markets in Financial Instruments Directive) has been of concern as it has not achieved what it set out to do, namely to improve trade execution by providing guarantees of processing in terms of the best price, cost, speed of processing. The fact that the Directive celebrates its third year of operation without a single major best execution case or fine shows how effective that has been, particularly as best execution is known to be way off. For example, Equiduct showed a year ago that of the €97 billion trades completed in January 2009 across the most liquid 500 stocks, a third (33.4%) could have achieved a better price on a different venue.

But other things have taken priority over best execution, such as survival and bonuses. So MiFID has failed in one of its core tenets. It has also failed in another: the transparency of trading.

According to a CFA Institute survey published last month, 68% of respondents felt that market fragmentation has created difficulties in trade reporting obligations.

Although the survey finds no empirical evidence that the fragmentation of trading and pricing has been detrimental to price formation, it does highlight the number one issue for most market constituents, which is the need for a consolidated tape for quote and trade data for European equity markets. You see, there are so many trading venues now, each reporting their trades to their own chosen public reporting sites, that users have to increase their connectivity to a much wider range of venues than ever before. With each connection costing around £10,000 per month, that's a high cost.

This concern has been picked up by Thomson Reuters, which has produced an interesting white paper on European data consolidation this month. It provides three key conclusions:

- "The buy side considers the cumulative cost of fees charged by exchanges and trade reporting services is a significant barrier to adoption of a consolidated tape, and a detriment to overall transparency. We suggest there should be a more modular approach to data pricing that is underpinned by regulatory intervention.
- "The coverage and quality controls around MiFID trade publication need to be formalised and enforced to instil market confidence and trust. We make several suggestions to improve trade publication. To be successful, the institutional buy side, brokers and trade reporting services will need to reach agreement on standards, and these rules will need to be codified through MiFID 2 regulation.
- "Best execution monitoring has been hampered by shortcomings in the provision of the source data contributing to a consolidated tape and by inconsistencies of approach to benchmark calculation between information vendors.

> In this document, we openly share our TCA (Transaction Cost Analysis) formulas and methodology. We now call upon other vendors to join in defining industry standards for data consolidation and TCA measurement."

The consolidated tape is the priority for MiFID 2 therefore, along with sorting out the issues of best execution and pricing.

What else might be in there? Dark pools?

Sure, they are a big issue, aren't they? The CFA survey found that 70% believe dark pools are problematic for price discovery, and the Federation of European Stock Exchanges (FESE) estimates that as much as 40% of trading takes place in the dark. That means the general investor does not get to see these prices and orders until they are filled in a 'hidden' dark world. FESE says that is wrong.

The banks say it's just the exchanges trying to create a smokescreen and that there's no way the trading in dark pools is at that sort of level. In fact, the FSA has found that it is only about 2.5% of OTC trades that take place through dark pools whilst, across Europe, CESR estimates it to be more like 1.25%.

Between the MTF impacts, the increasing use of dark pools, the lack of consistent trade reporting, the increasing use of flash orders and high frequency trading, the need for best execution and price transparency, and more, the regulators have still got a lot on their plate for this MiFID review. Crisis or no crisis.

MiFID Wave 2 (2010)

A colleague from Credit Agricole's subsidiary, CA Cheuvreux, sent me a really interesting white paper on the MiFID review and has kindly given me permission to post it here.

"Issues linked to Crossing Engines (internal order crossing systems) can only be properly understood after a review of the new landscape that emerged following MiFID. We witnessed a destructuring of the market, which has resulted in a war of tick sizes and the emergence of a new category of entrants favoured by the pricing set up by exchanges. During this period, traditional players saw their costs soar, a factor that could lead to the exit of the weakest players without sufficient financial wherewithal to cope with the expenses resulting from MiFID. Pre-transparency, which was one of the major vectors of MiFID, has deteriorated, and liquidity on the lit markets has become an illusion. It is precisely the deterioration of the quality of the lit side that has driven participants to increase their use of dark venues (dark part of MTFs and Crossing Engines) in order to protect the interests of clients wishing to access all liquidity pools. Concerns that subsequently rose regarding price formation mechanisms cannot be lifted by regulating dark pools indiscriminately but rather by restoring the quality of the lit world."

The return of the MiFIDs, 2010-2012+ (2010)

We had a fun meeting of the Financial Services Club this week, looking at the implications of MiFID and the outlook for MiFID 2.

We now see more developments taking place, including investigations by CESR – the Committee of European Securities Regulators – that will conclude at the end of May 2010 and covers 107 questions across a broad spectrum of issues:

Investor protection and intermediaries

- Telephone recording;
- Execution data quality;
- Instrument complexity;
- Personal recommendations;
- Supervision of tied agents;
- Options and discretions.

Equity markets

- Pre-trade regime for RM/MTFs;
- Definition of Sis;
- Post trade transparency regime;
- Extended scope of transparency;
- Regulatory framework for consolidation and cost of market data;
- RM and MTF alignment and crossing networks;
- Eliminating options and discretions.

Transaction reporting

- New trading capacity (riskless principal);
- Counterparty and client identifiers;
- User guidelines (how to fill in the reports).

There are also bigger issues, such as the post-trade clearing environment and its challenges. For some time, there has been reference to a Clearing and Settlement Directive for example, and MiFID 2 is meant to address this.

It is also meant to address the fragmentation of trade reporting and the price tape. It may also pop a whack at 'dark pools' and high frequency trading. For all we know, it could even re-regulate the new electronic trading platforms – most of which are yet to wipe their face with a profit – and make them completely unworkable by introducing reporting rules and overheads that are as onerous as the ones that traditional stock exchanges have to work with.

Now, to be clear, we don't know what's in MiFID 2 right now – we won't really know until 2012 or after when the new regulation is drafted. Meanwhile, there are some rapid fire changes ahead with key dates this year including:

- April: The FSA formed a MiFID working party and trade associations, such as FIX Protocol, ISITC, FISD and RDUG all have meetings looking at the implications of MiFID 2.

- May: CESR hearings on key questions and issues around MiFID2 and closure of consultation at end of month.
- June: The MiFID JWG, Joint Working Group, reforms on 9th June in a meeting at Thomson Reuters.

Wow! The MiFID JWG reforms. Can't wait to be there ...

MiFID's progress: slow, but sure (2009)

It's been two years since MiFID came into force in Europe and not a great deal has changed in the world of European trading... or has it? There are certainly new exchanges and new clearing systems, but the general landscape of Europe dominated by the three largest exchanges – Deutsche Bourse, NYSE Euronext and the London Stock Exchange – remains unfazed ... or is it? Certainly there are many pretenders to these giants' thrones, but are any of them really up to the job?

In November 2007, MiFID's rules on transparency of trading came into force. The idea was that we would have a pan–European investment market that would be as open and seamless as the US markets. Various players threw their hat into the ring to shake things up and, two years later, only one is making any major inroads: the Instinet subsidiary, Chi-X. Meanwhile, the other pillar of MiFID's intent lies untested and unchallenged, namely the focus upon best execution. However, for anyone to believe that MiFID is a damp squib would be wrong. It has shaken the foundations of the European investment industry by bringing in new technologies, new focus and new pricing systems that, over time, will demonstrate a radical restructuring of the European markets.

Before we delve deep into this territory, let's look at the new competition first.

The first mover to leverage MiFID's opportunities was Chi-X, the pan-European equities exchange geared towards algorithmic trading. The fact that Chi-X was first mover, opening for business in April 2007, meant that by the time the second movers came into the market – Turquoise and NASDAQ OMX started trading effectively in September 2008 – there had been an 18-month cycle of gaining liquidity which has proven hard to break.

Under MiFID's rules, there is meant to be a requirement for best execution based upon the price, speed and cost of processing, but this rule has never been tested and, more often than not, trades flow to where the market knows. Therefore, Deutsche Bourse, NYSE Euronext and the LSE are still thriving, and the only new entrant to make any headway has been Chi-X.

Chi-X claims that this is based upon more than just being first mover, as they do offer very low latency (high speed) capabilities for high frequency traders. For example, the cycle time to process an order through Chi-X is around two milliseconds, compared to around six for Turquoise and significantly slower cycles through the traditional exchanges.

This low latency capability has been critical for the main market makers, who see speed of trading as a key factor for exploiting market opportunities and leveraging their algorithmic trading systems.

In addition, the second movers launch in September 2008 was just bad timing as this coincided with the market crash caused by Lehman Brothers collapse. Launching new equities exchanges just as all market trading volumes declined significantly was just poor timing.

It does not mean that the new entrants and market restructuring has finished though, as other trading facilities have launched since September 2008, including Equiduct, BATS and Quote MTF. In fact, according to the Council of European Securities Regulators (CESR, soon to become the European Securities

Authority), there are 125 Multilateral Trading Facilities (MTFs) that have registered for licence with them since MiFID came into force.

And most of these facilities have one thing in common: low latency technologies at low cost.

For example, the average order cycle, including clearing, is 10 basis points on the new exchanges, compared with 70 or more on the old exchanges. They also have a model based upon a higher fee for those who take liquidity versus those who bring liquidity. Finally, they are highly geared towards dark pool trading activities and electronic liquidity providers through advanced technology services.

This last point is a key one as, alongside new equities exchanges, the other major change in European trading has been the rise of dark pools, where orders can sit waiting to be filled unseen. Turquoise was the first aggressive play in this space, backed as it is by the major market makers. Since Turquoise launched, we have seen several others rise including Smartpool from NYSE Euronext and Baikal from the LSE.

Nevertheless, these dark pools may encounter a few issues in the future as the USA is the model they are based upon, and Wall Street traders have recently found themselves in hot water over the use of dark pools and low latency to potentially manipulate the markets using flash trades, also known as 'gaming'. The way this works is that, through the automated systems for trading, dealers can see a large order entering an exchange a half a second before it is filled. That half a second allows them to rapidly process hundreds of orders for the shares about to be traded using algorithmic low latency processing. The result is that by the time the buyers' order is filled, the price has risen by a cent. Perform such trading regularly through the day, and those cents soon add up to a tidy profit for the brokers and dealers using such trading facilities.

These practices are about to be banned by the SEC, although NASDAQ has already said it will not allow them. Just as NASDAQ makes this announcement, NYSE Euronext's new data centre to support high frequency trading facilities is soon to open in the USA. Therefore, the market will move to support liquidity, and if the liquidity is legitimate then there will always be at least one exchange that will support it.

This is concerning the European Commission, even more so with the fact that pricing has become fragmented across so many pools of liquidity, many of which are dark. This is potentially the rule of unintended consequences and the rumours of a MiFID 2 to resolve these issues abound.

Meanwhile, all of this fragmentation and dark trading is having a major impact on the traditional exchanges.

The traditional exchanges spent many years protected by concentration rules that forced traders in each country to process orders through their national exchange. These rules were removed on November 1st 2007, when MiFID came into force, and has opened the exchanges to major new competitive forces unseen before.

Although these new competitors have struggled to take liquidity, the fact is that some are. Chi-X for example, is processing an average 20% of FTSE 100, DAX 30 and CAC40 shares these days, and Turquoise claims a further 5%, even nearing 10% of the FTSE 100.

A quarter or more of the most liquid shares trading on the traditional exchanges moving to the new exchanges in a couple of years is a concern, and each exchange has taken a different route to meet these concerns.

Deutsche Bourse saw a 7% drop in Xetra and 14% decline on Eurex trading in Q2 2009 compared with Q2 2008, with only Clearstream's custodial services delivering a bright spot. NYSE Euronext made a $182 million loss in Q2, mainly due to severance costs with LCH.Clearnet over their acquisition of LIFFE, the London-based derivatives exchange. And the LSE is in a right muddle, with former leader Dame Clara Furse leaving in a cloud of issues over their strategy and new CEO Xavier Role announcing a radical departure in approach.

The last point was the most shocking in fact, as ex-Lehman banker Xavier Role intimated that he was going to dump their flagship system, TradElect. TradElect was developed by Accenture and Microsoft as a next generation trading system that went live in the summer of 2007 at a cost of £40 million. The system was developed before the impact of dark pool and low latency trading however, and has never been able to compete with the order speeds of Chi-X and their clan.

Therefore, after only two years, the system looks to have had time called in order to create a real next generation trading service that processes at light speed.

Even so, one fact about the system has proven how difficult it is to take liquidity away from a trusted venue. Just before Lehman Brothers collapse, the LSE had a software failure for several hours on September 8th 2008. During this period, it should have led to major moves to the new exchanges as trading was stymied on the LSE for almost a day. It didn't happen however, because most of the pricing feeds at that time were tied to pricing on the LSE and, with no price feed from the LSE, there were no pricing deals to be done on the alternative exchanges.

This will change in due course, as the new players find their niche, but today it is still the case that most traditional exchanges own their markets, or a large part of their markets. Yes, it is being eroded, but only slowly.

Which brings me to a final point. The erosion of tradition exchanges dominance of their country's investments and trading is tied heavily to the openness and access to clearing and settlement in each constituency. Without easy securities settlement at the post-trade end of the process, the new exchanges are effectively frozen out of the markets.

The new exchanges have achieved a fair amount in resolving this issue, with new Central Counterparty (CCP) clearing systems from the USA, in the form of the EuroCCP a subsidiary of the DTCC, and in Europe with Fortis's European Multilateral Clearing Facility (EMCF). But there are still many issues in interoperability and access to clearing and settlement in many countries, as evidenced possibly by the strong results of Clearstream in the Deutsche Bourse's reporting this year.

Until the European Commission eradicates the Giovannini barriers – the barriers to cross-border securities settlement identified way back in 2003 and still unresolved today – and create a truly open and transparent post-trade system for Europe, the pre-trade equities exchanges can make inroads, but they will only be narrow roads rather than expressways.

In conclusion, two years after MiFID, Europe has a buoyant and lively marketplace for trading and investment that is gradually moving towards the European Commission's vision of an open and transparent pan-European trading regime. The new MTFs have managed to gain a quarter of the most liquid stocks trading activity, and this will grow even further over time. Meanwhile, the traditional exchanges are rethinking and redeploying new technologies to compete.

The result at this stage is that the liquidity pools of Europe are running deep ... and dark.

What has MiFID done for democracy? (2009)

I've had fascinating meetings with the Russian exchanges RTS and SPIMEX. You may wonder whether SPIMEX is something to do with finding out who started the swine flu pandemic but no, it's the St. Petersburg International Mercantile Exchange.

The two exchanges have very different start points and focal points, with RTS (the Russian Trading System) starting as a privately-owned exchange back in 1995, whilst SPIMEX is an initiative of the government to create a working commodities exchange.

I had been aware of RTS for a while as, during the MiFID investigations, their name came up many times as a working, highly automated exchange. Originally launched using NASDAQ's trading platform, they soon developed their own products and services, covering algorithmic trading for equities, forex, future and options and more.

Today, the exchange is one of the best performing, with the RTS Index tripling in value during 2009 to an index high of 1,451 at yesterday's close, compared to a market low back in February of under 500, although this is still well below the high of 2,487 in May 2008.

What is the reason for such volatility? Oil.

Chris Weafer, Chief Strategist at Uralsib Bank, puts it in context: "We've recovered very strongly this year mainly because of the recovery in the oil price. Plus, the recovery and optimism in the rest of the world has allowed for the Russian rouble to stabilise."

Or is it because RTS is a keen innovator offering analysis across every trader's portfolio and position in real-time, as the RTS people I spoke with yesterday said.

RTS now offers highly automated trading across 1,400 stocks, with 90% of the trades using automated systems and 10% OTC. It is also one of the top 40 global derivatives exchanges and trading is getting far more complicated, with around 15 trades per transaction on average today compared with 10 trades per transaction just two years ago.

Similarly, talking with the SPIMEX guys, there is a clear vision that they are trying to avoid being another failed commodities exchange (around 60 have been launched since 1990). Why did the previous exchanges fail? Because no-one trusted them, by the sound of it.

According to a SPIMEX advisor, it was because of a poor understanding of risk, a word rarely used because Russians do not allow risk to occur. This is why most exchange and exchanges are based upon 'fundamentals' – "if I can see it, touch it and trade it, then that's ok. If you are looking for me to pay now for something that might pay back in the future, no way."

This is why most Russian banks do not provide trade finance, and why oil is an issue.

For example, oil producers currently do not co-operate because they do not trust each other, according to one of the guys at SPIMEX.

Most oil producers are local monopolies with no competitive mechanisms. As a result, when oil prices rose in 2007–2008, Russians were paying more for their oil than America and Europe, even though Russia has more oil reserves and production than most.

So SPIMEX was launched in September 2008 to overcome this, with the Russian anti-monopoly committee creating the right environment to trade on exchange by fining several of the oil producers for anti-competitive practices.

But the real common feature of both SPIMEX and RTS is real-time risk management.

Both exchanges proudly talk about their focus upon real-time analysis of traders' positions. In the case of SPIMEX, they offer real-time settlement and straight through processing, so there is no risk for trading. In the case of RTS, they offer real-time positioning of every trader and every trader's clients portfolios, not just in real-time for their own trades but also for the knock-on effect of their dealings in derivatives down the line.

I asked RTS about their risk management, and they made clear that for each transaction, the risk is calculated for the trader's portfolio, including all orders to be filled, in real-time. There are then two clearing sessions during the day. One at 14:00, which takes three minutes to process, and the second is at end of day, and takes 15 minutes. If a margin call is made, the broker must cover their position within two hours or, if at end of day, before the start of the next day's trading.

This discussion got interesting, as RTS and SPIMEX appear to be developing systems that ensure no trader can leverage risk to the levels where the market implodes, and they do this in real-time.

It is the nature of new trading systems and operations that they design things to work in the ideal way, as the outline above is what Europe and USA are trying to develop.

For example, the FSA's £2 billion technology change program for real-time liquidity reporting is pretty much what RTS has today.

No wonder the gentleman from RTS turned to me towards the end of our chat and asked, straight-faced, "What has MiFID done for democracy?"

He probed me about best execution and what it means: "Is it just all about price, speed and cost (and likelihood of settlement)?"

I then realised what he was getting at. Where, in all the developments of MiFID and its best execution, transparency and competitiveness objectives, was the mention of risk? Where is the focus on real-time risk reporting?

Hmmmm ... it's obvious that RTS, and the Russian aspirations to build the next major Russian-Asian commodities exchange, is something to watch.

Meanwhile, the major thought that struck me in this dialogue, was that we have two opposites. In Europe and America, we have an over-leveraged, casino capitalism culture of trading that is now being re-engineered to restrain excessive risk without responsibility.

In Russia, we have a risk avoidance trading environment through real time controls, which needs to increase liquidity and leverage in order to fuel the flow of commerce.

If Russia does not achieve this, then its commodities ambitions cannot be achieved.

So maybe there is a happy medium here between the Russian approach to risk controls of trading, and the Anglo-Saxon approach of using financial instruments to create liquidity.

Now there would be a thought ...

Is it me or has CESR just screwed dark pools? (2010)

I had a meeting with a mate last night, who happens to be on the inside track of EU regulatory matters as they relate to capital markets; he turned to me and said: "Have you seen CESR's latest?" "What are they saying?" I asked. "Only that everyone now has to use EBBO!" he chortled.

EBBO is the European Best Bid-Offer pricing system. What does EBBO mean? It's basically a price that is dynamically updated with each change in the best price in any of the relevant markets where the instrument is traded. Therefore, if you're trading in HSBC or Vodafone, EBBO will look across all of the execution venues where those stocks are traded and will tell you the best bid and offer for those stocks in real-time.

So what is CESR saying? Looking at its website, it has updated MiFID with a new ruling on price waivers for execution venues as of this week (did anyone notice?).

Here's the exact text:

"Waivers from Pre-trade Transparency Obligations under the Markets in Financial Instruments Directive (MiFID) – updated 9th March 2010

(...)

All orders will be submitted to the system for execution/crossing at the midpoint of the European Best Bid and Offer (EBBO). The European Best Bid price is the highest binding bid (or buy) price available in the central limit order books of the regulated markets and MTFs contributing to the determination of the EBBO. The European Best Offer price is the respective binding lowest offer (or sell) price. Thus the EBBO will always deliver the tightest spread available in the contributing trading platforms."

The document says a lot more, but the heart of it seems to be getting at the opaqueness of pricing and lack of a single price feed. Hence, by enforcing a new rule whereby every participant has to guarantee Best Bid-Offer or – if crossing – the mid-point, they have wiped out much of the motivation for dark pool trading overnight.

Why? Because dark pools work at giving you a better spread than on the open market based upon a volume order, as well as allowing block trading unseen.

You want 1,000 HSBC or Vodafone stocks? Old days: you look at the markets and make a Visible Bid for them. If someone can trade at that price then they make a Visible Offer. New days: you place your order into a dark pool and it sits waiting to be filled at the price you specify, a Dark Bid. This bid is often a price that is better than on the open markets, e.g. not the European Best Bid-Offer but your, discounted Best Bid-Offer which can only be met by other 'dark' players who make a Dark Offer that is also unseen by the markets.

CESR's new ruling wipes out the new days overnight, as you are now only going to get that order filled by placing visible pricing levels. Or that's how my friend reads it.

Meanwhile, the question that arises is that Nomura and UBS have just launched into dark pool territories in the recent weeks ... has this just screwed their efforts big time?

Update as of 11th March

I've been pointed to references that the CESR rules allow Primary BBO (PBBO), and is not restricted to EBBO therefore. PBBO is explained well on Chi-X's website.

CESR has confirmed that PBBO is OK. Might have been worth them putting that in the document more clearly in my view, e.g. PBBO isn't mentioned once, but EBBO is everywhere.

And it still doesn't answer the basic question: by forcing dark pools to use mid point pricing for all trades undertaken removes the raison d'être as this gives bank-owned dark pools a significant reduction in spread, and therefore P&L, due to the price being a mid price set from an external source.

On the other hand, people like Nomura were fully aware of this. In fact, it's part of the reason for bringing NX to market.

So why would Nomura, Barclays and UBS make announcements and investments in dark pools if it gives them no major P&L advantage? It may be motivated by the need to access the LSE's Turquoise strategic steering committee ... and so the game rolls on.

My City friend agrees that Nomura understands what it needs to do in their MTF, but that the real issue is whether banks can still put their trading desk up as a counterparty to a customer order at anything other than a mid price?

This cuts to the heart of being a Systematic Internaliser, which none of them want to be and is the reason for the rush to be a dark MTF. However, if the rules are interpreted as above and all customer orders go into a dark pool, then the issue of where they are crossed with the prop book arises.

Does the FSA allow the prop book to cross a customer order outside the MTF or is it more likely that crossing with the prop book will need to be done within the MTF at the midpoint, which then cuts the P&L and internaliser gains?

More on CESR's dark pool regulations (2010)

I recently wrote a little piece about CESR, the EU Securities Regulator, and its update to dark pools regulations. It got quite a reaction, including feedback from some of the dark pools regulators themselves, who 'corrected' the view that the Best Bid-Offer had been updated by making it clear that nothing had actually changed recently.

For example, the document has been updated only to reflect how reference prices are formed in a negotiated trade waiver (Page 11). In fact, the clarification provided for me is that there are various price waivers allowed under MiFID:

The Reference Price Waiver

"This is allowed in various ways:

(a) All orders are submitted to the system for execution/crossing at the midpoint of the European Best Bid and Offer (EBBO); or

(b) All orders are submitted for execution/crossing at the midpoint of EBBO or the European Best Bid or the European Best Offer; or

(c) All orders are submitted for execution/crossing at the midpoint of the primary market BBO or the primary market's Best Bid or Best Offer; or

(d) All orders are matched and executed at the official closing price published by the primary market; or

(e) The trading platform offer continuous trading based on the volume weighted average price (VWAP) on the relevant primary market."

The Negotiated Trade Waiver

(This was the change made on March 9th.)

"In this case, the trading system formalises negotiated transactions at or within the volume weighted spread, so that trading participants individually agree on the price and volume of the trade before transmitting it to the trading platform. The system then ensures that all negotiated transactions are at or within the volume weighted spread on the public order book of the trading platform."

The Order Management Facility Waiver

"In this case the dark order system displays a part of the order (a peak) whilst the rest of the total volume of that order is not displayed, resting in the order management facility. After the displayed portion of the order has been executed, a new peak is sent to the order book with a new time stamp, and the non-displayed portion of the order is decreased accordingly."

The Large-in-Scale Waiver

"An order is 'large in scale' when compared with normal market size, if it is equal to or larger than the minimum size of order specified in Table 2 in Annex II of the Commission Regulation 1287/2006."

That last bit is complex and CESR can't agree on it, by the way. In fact, the whole darned lot is pretty complicated, but the point is that nothing much changed in recent days, apart from a new 'Negotiated Trade' Waiver.

What is clear is that this whole area will be under intense review when CESR draft MiFID 2.

The European Commission plans to expand MiFID trading rules to tackle issues missed by the original document, as calls mount for a second version of the controversial directive. The European regulator had been set to undertake a small-scale "technical" review of the 2007 directive, which outlawed rules forcing firms to use stock exchanges. However, sources familiar with the situation said the study might now include "more wide-ranging elements". Among changes that could be on the agenda are new rules on over-the-counter and structured products, a pulling together of trade-reporting requirements and tighter rules around the definition of 'best execution'.

How the Dodd-Frank legislation impacts capital markets (2010)

I just got this in my in-tray from Woodbine Associates, an American research firm that works with the exchange, broker/dealer, asset manager, hedge fund and technology vendor communities.

It's really interesting and talks about the impact the new American reforms, known as the Dodd-Frank Legislation, and how this law will impact the capital markets. Therefore, they've kindly given me permission to repurpose the material here.

How the law might really impact the capital markets

The Dodd-Frank Wall Street Reform and Consumer Protection Act has now become law. Interestingly, a wide range of opinion still exists as to how the law will impact financial markets and, not surprisingly, there is still a great deal of spin coming from various parties that seem more intent on unsettling the public than explaining the law. Dodd-Frank proponents applaud new consumer protection measures and rules focused on reducing systemic risk. Opponents of the law assert the legislation is likely to result in less consumer and small-business credit availability and that it will lead to the export of financial services jobs.

In our view, the Dodd-Frank law has a good chance of meaningfully impacting the financial markets by enhancing oversight, reducing systemic risk, and improving consumer protection. We discuss the first two points and highlight potential forthcoming market changes below.

Improved oversight

Dodd-Frank makes formidable strides in reducing regulatory oversight gaps. Some of the law's mandates are very straightforward and, we believe, can't help but improve regulators' ability to oversee market activity.

Some of the law's more notable elements in this vein include the creation of the Financial Stability Oversight Council (FSOC), placing of over-the-counter (OTC) derivatives under regulatory oversight, and reassigning particular responsibilities across various agencies within the oversight framework. Combined, these changes should go a long way to correcting various existing weaknesses and shortcomings.

Establishment of the FSOC should lead to better agency cohesion and improved coordination in implementing Dodd-Frank and new policy initiatives. One attractive aspect of the organization is that it will use resources already in place within the existing regulatory structure. Instead of creating yet another agency, this organization will unite talent from a range of existing organizations including the Treasury and Federal Reserve to identify and respond to issues pertaining to systemic risk in the financial system. The Council will also provide guidance to regulators in their respective markets.

OTC derivatives will be subject to regulatory oversight for the first time in history. While not reflecting the majority of transaction volume, OTC derivatives and highly structured products account for substantial market risk that, to this point, has not been monitored or measured on a market-wide level. Simply bringing visibility to this area of market activity is very likely to result in a clearer assessment of aggregate risk and leverage in the financial system.

Dodd-Frank also addresses certain deficiencies that exist in the current regulatory regime and redefines responsibility across a number of agencies. Without exploring those intricacies here, it suffices to say that the law reduces overlap and clarifies agency responsibilities rather than adding to or revamping the existing fragmented system.

Reduction in systemic risk

The new legislation is likely to lead to a notable reduction in systemic risk.

As we pointed out in our last Woodbine Opinion, the Volcker Rule will restrict bank investment in hedge funds to 3% of capital. An 11th hour compromise in Congress to pass the law diluted this aspect of the rule by changing the definition of 3% from "tangible" to "Tier 1" capital. Though slightly less stringent than the original provision, the measure still limits banks from potentially becoming heavily invested in risky hedge funds and indirectly putting the deposit base at risk.

In the same vein, the bank proprietary trading ban (which survived the legislative process intact) will substantially limit deposit-taking institutions from engaging in highly risky trading strategies for their own books. This will spell an end to large scale proprietary trading as it has existed at banks for the past 30 years and drive them to deposit services, extending credit, and client-oriented capital market business as their primary sources of revenue. Profits will decline as less glamorous but all-important commercial finance, retail lending, and account services become the central focus.

Equities

We expect the reduction in proprietary trading to have an adverse impact on equity market liquidity. However, the degree to which liquidity will be affected is unclear.

Proprietary trading formerly accounted for a significant portion of daily share volume. Although the trading landscape has changed in the past several years, the expansion of high frequency trading has caused a tremendous increase in trading volumes.

Accordingly, the adverse impact of declining liquidity due to the elimination of bank-related proprietary trading may well be offset by the benefits to market operations associated with high frequency trading. Recent data-based research we conducted ("The Impact of High Frequency Trading Highly Liquid US Equities" April, 2010) supported assertions that high frequency trading is beneficial to the market in a majority of the 39 most liquid US securities in that, on average, it improves execution quality and reduces volatility. We believe these favourable effects will "buffer" the impact of spread pressure resulting from the absence of bank proprietary trading in these 39 securities that, collectively, constitute approximately 20% of the daily market volume. However, the impact on spreads may be more keenly felt in smaller, more thinly traded securities. Without high-frequency trading to offset the decline in proprietary trading, the cost of raising equity capital through the public market could increase for smaller, less-established businesses.

Derivatives

Increased transparency in the derivatives markets resulting from Dodd-Frank should also be beneficial in terms of systemic risk reduction by placing specific controls around OTC derivatives. As has been previously noted, OTC derivatives contracts and most structured products are currently traded in a largely unregulated environment.

We believe the law will increase transparency and reduce credit exposure without significantly affecting the transfer of risk in the market. The new mandates will require large derivative trading firms to execute transactions electronically in an exchange or swap execution facility, clear through a clearinghouse, and report to a trade repository. Trades that are exempt from these requirements will face a higher capital charge, reflecting their additional risk. The resulting reduction in counterparty credit risk among trading partners is a significant element of the law's goal to reduce the inter-connectivity among major securities dealers.

The law also requires insured banks to spin off or "push out" non-hedging related derivative trading to separate affiliates. As this area becomes clarified by regulators, the ultimate impact on the market can be better discerned. As it stands, we expect that the impact will be largely organizational, with associated capital implications. We do not expect this provision to significantly affect trading.

The combination of electronic markets, clearing, and reporting will add significantly to market depth and liquidity. This will level the playing field for less creditworthy counterparties and foster greater price competition among a larger group of market makers. Less liquid products, such as some of the more esoteric credit default swaps (CDSs) and collateralized debt obligations (CDOs), stand the most to gain in terms of price discovery and spread compression.

Fixed income

Almost nothing in the law, outside of the ban on bank-related proprietary trading, will directly affect overall operation of the

US fixed income market. Specific areas will be impacted, such as asset backed securitization where underwriters are required to retain 5% of the credit risk in originated securities. A similar risk retention requirement will exist for certain types of non-exempt residential mortgage backed securities as well; however, the securities that will be affected have yet to be determined. We believe that this will be positive for the markets as underwriters will now have some "skin in the game," increasing their due diligence.

New accountability facing credit rating firms (including legal liability to investors for their ratings) should bolster their accuracy and independence and restore some confidence in their assessment of creditworthiness. This should be a welcomed change since credit rating arbitrage, coupled with insufficient investor due diligence, played a significant role leading up to the structured credit market meltdown.

Perhaps the most interesting part of the law with respect to the fixed income market will be the effect that electronic trading of fixed income derivatives has on the underlying cash markets. We believe movement toward more robust electronic trading is inevitable for most fixed income securities as the efficiencies derived from current technology are too overwhelming to be ignored. More advanced electronic trading is currently conducted almost exclusively among the major market participants. Forthcoming changes to the derivatives market may well provide the catalyst for more widespread adoption of electronic trading.

Reduction in bank lending largely hype

We are not clear how opponents to the Dodd-Frank law purport that reform will lead to a decline in the availability of business and retail credit. The best we can determine is that they believe that greater regulation will raise business cost for smaller lending institutions, driving some out of business, and resulting in less available, more expensive credit for small businesses and less creditworthy individuals, from fewer banks.

The business cost argument is not new. In our experience, it has been one of the most widely used arguments against regulation when opponents lack reasonable or rational grounds upon which to object. We have yet to see any bank, broker, exchange, ECN, or ATS be truly hurt through compliance-oriented spending in connection with new regulation.

We think the cost argument is largely hype that could be traced to banks intent on protecting their bottom line. In other words, the cost argument is really an indirect objection to impending revenue reductions likely to result from the new legislation. In fact, once the legislation is implemented, bank operating models may very well resemble those at banks between the 1930s and 1990s while the Glass-Steagall Act was in place.

Glass-Steagall prohibited deposit-taking institutions from underwriting and trading in equity securities. During this period, widespread derivatives trading, for the most part, was non-existent. Banks focused their business efforts on account services and lending. Guess what? Business was just fine.

Job export

We agree with Dodd-Frank opponents that the new legislation is likely to result in firms shifting certain financial services positions overseas. A more restrictive business environment may well result in so-called "regulatory arbitrage," in which firms move business activities to less restrictive markets. Some trading will, no doubt, find its way to such geographies.

In regard to the potential export of jobs, we ask the fundamental question: Does it make sense to forgo beneficial legislation in the interest of repatriating a limited number of financial services positions?

We believe the answer is a resounding "no."

We are not insensitive to those who have or may lose employment. However, it is what is natural and necessary during periods of structural economic change. Changes short of those mandated by the law would simply preserve a flawed business environment to protect the interests of a few. Preserving a flawed system to retain a relatively small number of jobs potentially places our nation's economic engine and standard of living at risk.

In all, we believe that the Dodd-Frank Wall Street Reform and Consumer Protection Act is a remarkable piece of legislation that is bound to bring about beneficial changes to the financial markets. While no legislation is perfect and, no doubt, there are certain to be meaningful issues surrounding the law, we are impressed that legislators held their ground and retained important substance necessary to correct flaws in financial market operations. It is always easier to repeal rules than to implement them. Let's hope this law helps achieve the best balance of our free market engine and social objectives.

Europe's new regulatory agenda (2010)

We had a fascinating and packed meeting at the Financial Services Club this week with David Doyle, EU Policy Advisor, discussing the challenges of the new Barosso European Parliament and their legislative drive in financial services.

David is a regular visitor to the Financial Services Club, and runs our European Financial Regulatory Advisory Group. In a broad and wide ranging speech, he presented key views around MiFID, the PSD, Solvency II, UCITS IV, Basel III and more, as well as commentary on Jacques de Larosière's committee and the appointment of Michel Barnier to succeed Charlie McCreevy.

Here's a summary of the key points David made.

The Commission is taking a 'safety first approach' to regulating capital markets and market actors, and will fill in the gaps where European or national regulation is insufficient or incomplete.

The over-riding principles of their approach are that:

- All that is of systemic importance should be regulated and supervised;
- There is a need for a better well-capitalised finance industry, with less leverage;
- The Commission must legislate to avoid the perverse incentives in the financial sector that encourage excessive risk-taking or over-reward;
- Supervision should have the right tools to grasp complex, inter-connected and globalised financial activities; and
- To restore trust, investors and consumers should benefit from clearer, more coherent and effective safeguards.

At this point, audience members asked lots of questions about whether the European approach would be the same as, or co-ordinated with, the US approach. David's feeling is that it is being co-ordinated on the big ticket items – risk, leverage, capital, bonuses and such like – but the rest is still open competition in terms of the way payments, capital markets and specific aspects of the market are operating, such as hedge funds.

There are then the key changes that should be introduced by the new Barosso team in the near term as a result of the Jacques de Larosière. Of these changes, David believes that the new supervisory bodies will be the key here:

- European Securities and Markets Authority (ESMA);
- European Banking Authority (EBA);
- European Insurance and Occupational Pensions Authority (EIOPA).

These new authorities will have teeth, and will be responsible for ensuring that any EU member states which are not following the line of regulatory oversight are brought to order.

This will be in play within two years:

- **2009-2010** National FSA powers strengthened plus focus on harmonising national rules to reduce cross-border differences;
- **2011-2012** Implement pan-EU supervision via ESMA/ EBA/EIOPA,

and will mean that the large states which are proactively interpreting directives will be in a far stronger position than those states resisting such supervision. In practice, this means the UK, Netherlands are going to be fine; France and Germany will have some wrinkles to iron out; other nations will get a note to say they need to fine tune some stuff; and Spain and Italy will get a large wet fish slapped around their chops. After all, with every directive I deal with – MiFID and the PSD in particular – it's Spain and Italy which always seem to be dragging their heels.

David also made an interesting point here, which is that not only will the new regulatory bodies have teeth to drag member states before Brussels to explain why they are dragging their heels, but also resources to assist when assistance is needed. Therefore, in the case of Sweden where their key person for transposition of the PSD left at a critical juncture, this future structure would allow the EBA – the European Banking Authority, which is not to be confused with the EBA, the Euro Banking Association, that operates STEP2 and EURO1 – to provide people to fill the gaps. These people may be promoted in from regulatory authorities in other EU member states for example and, in so doing, it will fill the gaps.

David then rifled through all of the areas for legislation and key directives including:

- The Payment Services Directive;
- MiFID and Market Abuse updated rules;
- Capital requirements Directive III & IV;
- Remuneration;

- Pan-EU Supervisory Mechanisms;
- Hedge Funds & Private Equity;
- OTC Derivatives;
- Solvency II – Insurance;
- Responsible Lending & Borrowing;
- Packaged Retail Investment Products;
- UCITs IV;
- Credit Rating Agencies.

It was real insight and incredibly useful stuff.

A new EU regulatory structure (2009)

There has been a conference in Brussels over the last two days looking at moving towards a new supervisory architecture across Europe. This follows on from the de Larosière report in February and Charlie McCreevy has announced a variety of changes in EU regulatory structures.

In one speech, Mr. McCreevy reinforces the need for the 5% rule in securitisation:

> "On the now famous '5% retention' for securitisation, I'm pleased to see that the Parliament has resisted the call from industry to do away with what they had only last year characterised as complete non sense. I am delighted to say that the retention rule has emerged as something that is not non sense but plain 'common sense'. It is now recognised by G20 as a key measure to strengthen the financial system."

In a second, he announces two critical changes to supervisory structures:

> "In line with the de Larosière recommendations, we will soon present the details of an enhanced European financial supervisory framework based on two new pillars:

> "The first pillar is the European Systemic Risk Council (ESRC), which has been discussed this morning. This Council will monitor and assess the risks to the stability of the financial system as a whole. It would provide early warning of systemic risks and, where necessary, present recommendations for action to address these risks.
>
> "The creation of this Council would address one of the fundamental weaknesses highlighted by this crisis, which is the exposure of the financial system to interconnected, complex, sectoral and cross-sectoral systemic risks.
>
> "The second pillar is the creation of the European System of Financial Supervisors (ESFS) consisting of a network of national supervisors working in tandem with the new European Supervisory Authorities.
>
> "The new European network will be built on shared and mutually reinforcing responsibilities, combining nationally based supervision of firms with the centralisation of specific tasks at the European level. The driver behind the network is to foster harmonised rules as well as coherent supervisory practice and enforcement."

And in a third speech, Charlie directs fire at the accounting systems leading up to this crisis:

> "The IASCF is now the powerhouse for world accounting and this must be reflected in its governance structure. Whilst we fully acknowledge the IASCF's achievements to date in reforming its governance structure, notably the introduction of the Monitoring Board, there are a number of issues which still require action:
>
> - The geographic composition of IASB board members: there should be a greater link with the countries that actually apply IFRS;

- Proper due process: the importance of consultations, due process and feedback should not be underestimated; and
- A balanced Board with members with more practical experience and not just theoreticians."

I then notice a press release that says that "The Governing Council of the European Central Bank (ECB) has today decided that the European Investment Bank (EIB) will become an eligible counterparty in the Eurosystem's monetary policy operations on 8 July 2009."

Not making too many connections, but between TARGET2 and the other ECB controls; central clearing for OTC derivatives alongside a central code of conduct for pan-European clearing and settlement; a systemic risk council and supervisory group for Europe and more control for CEIOPS, CEBS and CESR; and all the other things happening in Brussels, the bottom line is: expect big changes to come!

Why regulators find it so hard to regulate (2009)

I hosted a fascinating dinner last night which built upon the comments made yesterday about regulators being unable to regulate.

The theme was around how to make the G20 supervisory framework work with regulators, compliance heads, bank directors and a CIO in attendance. All in all, a nice crowd, and a convivial conversation.

However, I did note a few comments such as:

"Europe is run by the Council of Ministers";

"European regulations are overly prescriptive";

"Greed is the biggest desire and how do you regulate that?"

"I'm amazed by the financial regulator's lack of teeth";

"The French make the laws as complex as possible and then don't follow them".

Oh yes, nothing like being a London-based European is there?

Now this may sound like a disaffected group, but it isn't. It is more a case that you can create as many rules and laws as you like but if they are unclear, unworkable or inappropriate, then you cannot enforce them.

This is the frustration of the regulators as much as the regulated, and there is no simple answer.

We then talked about principles- versus rules-based regulation, with three-quarters of the room saying that principles-based regulation is still far more appropriate than rules-based. Although rules are easier to follow, they can be too constraining.

Then the conversation was pulled up by the statement that principles-based regulation no longer works and we should focus upon outcomes-based regulation.

Interesting, especially as we have a lengthy process of new outcomes-based regulation coming through, such as the FSA's Consultation Paper entitled 'Strengthening liquidity standards 2: Liquidity reporting' (CP09/13) released yesterday.

I haven't had time to read the document but PJ Di Giammarino, who chairs the Financial Services Club's Capital Markets Chamber, posted a commentary as follows:

"After a rapid review of the 174-page CP09/13 response on liquidity reporting, we think the FSA is essentially saying 'We appreciate it is going to be hard but get on with it, because we are serious'.

"Despite many of the 98 respondents to the 15 questions in CP 08/22 (the first consultation paper released last December) highlighting the practical issues associated in delivering new reports, the FSA has decided that liquidity problems need to be monitored daily. And for banks this means exactly what it says on the tin.

"The FSA recognises that reporting requirements may be costly to implement but believes the data concerned would normally be utilised by most firms during the normal course of business.

"In an important nod to the recent G20 meeting, it is also clear that the FSA is engaged in international efforts to align other regulators to its data-intensive approach – and then use this as the basis of cross-border benchmarks.

"Firms should expect the new rules and guidance to be in effect in the fourth quarter of this year with new FSA reporting arrangements going live in Q1 2010. It goes without saying that there's a huge amount of work to be done across the industry to get this right.

"Our discussions with practitioners in banks lead us to conclude that, whilst much of this makes good business sense, it has the consequence of asking banks to rethink their infrastructures from the bottom up. The good news is that investment firms now have a clear and certain regulatory target to aim at."

This also builds on the De Larosière report and other rulings, and my take on PJ's comments is that the FSA has placed stringent rules in play which will force banks to report daily based upon strong liquidity data analysis.

Sounds like a prescriptive regulation if you ask me, and promotes the idea that outcomes-based regulation is not going to be based on principles but will be based upon strong controls, enforceable through prescriptive data reporting structures.

A-ha ... and hopefully with teeth and co-ordination for a consistent approach across geographies.

But even if it isn't, it does not matter as the key here is to have a transparent regulatory environment which ensures a robust marketplace, and the more robust the marketplace the more market players.

It honestly doesn't matter what the UK, France, Germany, Spain, Italy or others implement in their interpretation of EU Directives, it just matters that each creates a strong and robust marketplace which attracts liquidity and has some form of consistency, even if not quite 100% the same.

This is why the FSA always jumps in first, because they want the UK market to be the most robust and well regulated, to encourage participation in that market over others.

And there's the rub. Who can create the market that has great regulations, which are easy to work with and robust, whilst avoiding constraints and rules which might deter business and liquidity. And one, of course, that averts a disaster anything like the one we've just experienced in this crisis.

Anyways, back to the dinner and the comment that resonated the loudest around the room was the one that asked: "Where's the customer's voice?"

In all the dialogue about regulations and regulating, the focus appears to have been to lock the horse back in the barn after its bolted whilst the fact is that the farm still needs looking after.

In other words, are we focusing too much upon the crisis and its issues, or should we be focusing back on what is good for corporations and citizens, and then apply this to the banks?

I guess we're trying to do both: to plug the holes in our existing legislation that allowed the credit bubble to balloon and burst, whilst protecting corporations and customers from past, current and potential future misdemeanours.

No wonder the regulators have such a hard time.

Can regulators really regulate? (2009)

David Doyle, expert on all things in finance with a Brussels flavour, and I regularly tag-team on MiFID and the PSD, and in the wider context of Europe's Financial Services Action Plan.

In particular, he has an inside track on all this stuff and presented the latest updates on Europe's Directives at the Financial Services Club Ireland last week.

What struck me as David outlined the massive change agenda in plan, is that the process of drafting regulations is fine ... but can any of this work? Answer: probably not.

First, there are all the local regulations, such as Faster Payments in the UK. Then there are the national implementations of European regulations already in play, such as the PSD.

These all have slight variations in that every country's policymakers have a different view of how the PSD impacts their national banking structures.

(...)

Then there is the EU process of evolving regulations for Capital Adequacy and Solvency II, UCITS IV, Retail Investment Products, Market Abuse and more.

Finally, there is now the global agenda of the G20 to create consistent supervision across regions as well as within regions. So far, this has been an aggressive and very broad agenda in the EU.

As David made clear last week, the Commission is taking a 'safety first approach' to regulating capital markets and market actors, filling in the gaps where European or national regulations are insufficient or incomplete. In particular, these will be created for:

- **Credit rating agencies** (April 2009);

- **Hedge funds and private equity:** to include private equity and other systemically important market players (April 2009);
- **Crisis prevention:** a White Paper on tools for early intervention to prevent a crisis (June 2009);
- **Derivatives:** a report on derivatives and other complex structured products will provide a basis for Commission initiatives to increase transparency and ensure financial stability (June 2009);
- **Prudential capital:** legislative proposals to increase the quality and quantity of trading-book activities and tackle complex securitisation (Due: June 2009), and to address liquidity risk and excessive leverage (Autumn 2009).

In addition, there is a rolling program to update and create a far more consistent approach to global and European supervisory rules.

But I just cannot see all of this working, and beg the question: can regulators really regulate such a broad and aggressive agenda, or are they smoking dope?

It took us 10 years to develop the European Financial Services Action Plan, and where did we get to? A vast array of Directives which some countries implement and some do not. These Directives have attacked the simplistic areas of retail financial products, insurance, payments and investing. Now, with the credit crisis and the realisation of the complexity of global derivatives, we are tackling the complex financial areas of exotic options, futures, clearing and settlement.

So how does this work? How can a regulator create global, regional and national rules that are all harmonised, consistent, integrated and cooperative? What happens when countries, such as Costa Rica, opt out?

These are all the tough questions for the regulators and policymakers to answer but, my own view ... no matter how much regulation the governments of the world draft and create to address this crisis and harmonise rules:

(a) Can they be implemented?
(b) Can they be enforced?
(c) Are they truly global and how do you deal with countries that are non-cooperative?
(d) Are they water-tight or can market operators wriggle around them?

... and more. Not throwing rocks or anything, as we do need regulatory enforcement, but I would suggest that:

(a) It is still light touch, as detail will constrain implementation;
(b) It is enforced via regional and global cooperation of the G20;
(c) The G20 and United Nations sanction nations that are uncooperative;
(d) If it is light touch, then it is not water-tight but should be clear enough that any non-compliant market operator is hounded out of the markets by other market operators being whistleblowers about their bad behaviours.

Whoops. Did I say that they should be whistleblowers? Hound out the non-compliant market operators? No way. After all, the role of most market makers is to find ways to create risk to make money, not to be compliant with the rules.

I guess the answer really needs to be that the regulators and policymakers are clued up enough about the complexity of these markets that they can slap down any non-compliant performers before they create another bubble such as the leveraged debt of the credit default swaps markets.

And how do they do that? By being intimate with all market operations from the simple to the complex, not just the way they've behaved to date which is to hire administrators who can draft rules about the simple stuff.

European regulators scramble to plug the gaps (2009)

David Doyle, policy expert on European financial markets, discussed the latest European financial services legislative movements at the Financial Services Club yesterday.

David began with an outline of the priorities for the Czech Presidency of the European Union, which runs through to June:

- Review of the Capital Requirements Directive for the capital adequacy of investment firms and credit institutions;
- Negotiations of the Solvency II Directive regulating the insurance sector;
- Regulation of credit rating agencies;
- A new Directive for electronic money institutions;
- Review of the regulation on cross-border payments in euro;
- Review of the Market Abuse Directive;
- A New Prospectus Directive;
- UCITS IV; and
- Updating the International Financial Reporting Standards (IFRS).

I guess having so many priorities is not surprising, given the events of the past six months, but this list is too long and the priorities are too many. Therefore, David focused upon the changes to Solvency II and the revised Capital Requirements Directive (CRD).

These are significant changes to the original implementation of Basel II in Europe. For example, the new rules for the CRD were put forward on 1st October 2008, two weeks after Lehman Brothers collapse:

> "The European Commission has put forward a revision of EU rules on capital requirements for banks that is designed to reinforce the stability of the financial system, reduce risk

exposure and improve supervision of banks that operate in more than one EU country. Under the new rules, banks will be restricted in lending beyond a certain limit to any one party, while national supervisory authorities will have a better overview of the activities of cross-border banking groups. The proposal, which amends the existing Capital Requirements Directives, reflects extensive consultation with international partners, Member States and industry. It now passes to the European Parliament and the Council of Ministers for consideration."

The critical changes include improving the:

- Management of large exposures, particularly by introducing restrictions in interbank exposures;
- Supervision of cross-border banking groups through a collegiate of supervisors;
- Assessment of the quality of banks' capital through 'hybrid' capital rules Incorporating both equity and debt elements;
- Liquidity risk management: for banking groups that operate in multiple EU countries; and
- Risk management for securitised products through new rules on securitised debt.

There are some major points raised here. For example:

- The concept that banks must not be allowed to lend more than 25% of the their capital;
- That regulators across all markets work together to monitor the activities of key cross-border groups and, bearing in mind that over 70% of all cross-border activities are transacted by only 45 financial institutions, this may mean more stringent regulation through both home and host oversight;

- A need to retain a minimum 5% of capital for anything that is securitised, with some still asking for this to be raised to 15%.

The thing is that this is all being fast-tracked, with the intention of sign off in the European Parliament for the revised CRD by April 2009. That's fast, and raises the concerns of irrational and ill-thought through regulation, rather than better regulation. However, bearing in mind that there are MEP elections in June and a new Commission selected in November, when Charlie McCreevy leaves office, and you can see why they want to get this through in time for implementation.

David proceeded to analyse developments in other areas, such as:

- The EU's divergent policies on credit rating agencies, who will be banned from providing any advisory services as well as providing complete transparency of the models, methodologies and key assumptions on which they base their ratings;
- The Electronic Money Directive which will enforce same day payments for euro-based direct debits and credit transfers, but will not apply to mobile operators (why not?); and
- The fact that the Commission now has hedge funds and private equity in their line of sight, as well as short selling and dark pool equities trading, with a new Directive likely to target this area.

David's analysis was wide and deep, which is the reason why I invited him to address our meeting. He concluded with the fact that there are estimated to be 123 regulatory supervisors across the EU, who will now work as a collegiate to enforce these rules under a single EU Regulatory Authority.

The single EU regulatory authority has been a challenge for a long time, and with recent developments looks increasingly likely.

We finished the evening with questions that focused upon principles-based versus rules-based regulations; the world after Charlie McCreevy and whether there will be big changes if a non-Northern Commissioner is selected; Davos, the G8 and the G20, and the whole challenge of domestic versus regional versus global regulatory co-ordination.

The conclusion is that regulators are scrambling to plug the gaps and issues created in recent days. Their fast-track actions may not be the right ones long-term but are the necessary ones for the short term.

Chapter 3 The liquidity debate

The
Complete
Banker

Introduction

When Lehman Brothers collapsed in September 2008, it led to a huge amount of distrust between banks. The reason was that almost $10 trillion of derivatives trading related in some way to Lehman Brothers' good name in the form of credit default swaps (CDS). The collapse meant that nearly every bank stopped trusting their counterparties and the risks between each other. That is really bad for investment markets, where liquidity is based upon having easy access to funds and complete trust. Liquidity is therefore critical today, and liquidity risk is a new area of risk that has been identified in the markets. In fact, you can confidently state that liquidity – access to funds when needed – is today's and tomorrow's big issue.

FSA liquidity regime in jeopardy (2009)

PJ Di Giammarino, Chairman of the Financial Services Club's Capital Markets Chamber, released his firm's findings about liquidity views in the City today.

PJ's company, JWG-IT, polled over 30 financial institutions and 10 vendors on their implementation readiness for the FSA's new rulings in the spring and twice more in July.

The results showed that banks are not ready for the new liquidity regime, and that the FSA's attempts to set and communicate an actionable implementation plan for liquidity risk have so far failed.

Part of the issue appears to be the differing opinions on how to run the banks in the future, with disagreements between the FSA, Bank of England and Treasury causing uncertainty of approach.

That's fine, except that the FSA's aggressive timescales now leave banks less than 75 work days to implement a data-intensive approach to liquidity risk management. Bearing in mind that their own estimates show that the price tag for this regime will be well in excess of £2 billion, that's a problem.

JWG-IT's research found that senior management within banks are only just beginning to understand the magnitude of the upgrades required for liquidity risk. The main findings from the research include:

- **Awareness:** Only 41% had heard of the FSA's liquidity risk standards consultation paper (CP 08/22) which were released in December 2008;
- **Systems:** 64% of 20 bank respondents indicated that their existing systems could not be easily adapted to the new liquidity requirements;
- **Data quality:** 41% of bank respondents indicated that meeting liquidity data requirements would be their biggest implementation challenge;
- **Controls:** 33% of respondents ranked liquidity risk systems and controls as their top issue - carrying the highest risk and requiring the most resource to resolve;
- **Resources:** 28% of respondents indicated that no resources had been allocated to their top 3 issues of scenario/stress testing, risk modelling/analytics and data.

For further information see JWG-IT's analysis report, 'Winning the risk governance battle'.

FSA Liquidity Rules – a threat to London banks' global role? (2009)

Tom Groenfeldt attended our recent meeting of the Financial Services Club, where the new FSA Liquidity Rules were debated. Here's his report:

The FSA's new rules on liquidity management threaten to overload banks with reporting that the regulator won't be able to understand while missing the source of the current financial crisis, said panellists at the Financial Services Club Capital Markets forum.

Because the session was conducted under Chatham House rules, this commentary doesn't identify individual speakers. There was broad agreement that the FSA's new rules, which are to take effect in October, largely miss the cause of the current problems.

Panellists agreed that banks are holding onto liquidity to survive.

"What kills a bank? If it loses liquidity it dies. The essence of why banks aren't lending to banks isn't any longer about counterparty trust. It is banks thinking they need a liquidity buffer that is bigger than in the past – if there is a run they want to make sure they can pay everything they owe on the dot." The American program to offer insurance is a useful approach to improving liquidity.

National regulators threaten to undermine international banks because they focus just on performance within the nation's borders.

"How can the FSA or any national regulator adequately regulate multinational institutions when all they do is look at the local part of that institution? If Asia is in trouble the FSA may ignore I,t but the bank with operations in Asia won't." Regulators will simply want to ensure a bank is self-sufficient in its home country, but that won't work in a global world.

"If you trap liquidity in your own system, how does the UK function as an international centre?" Parliament appears to want finance to shrink to the national borders, said another speaker. The FT has reported that the FSA's proposals are under fire from the financial services industry.

"The FSA's proposals would force banks to hold greater reserves of government bonds than in the past. It would also force

UK subsidiaries of foreign banks to be self-sufficient in terms of funding, unless their parent companies met certain criteria."

The FSA stressed that its proposals were subject to consultation and that it was supportive of efforts to come up with a global solution to the problem, said the FT.

At the FS Club, participants suggested delaying implementation of the rule for six to nine months.

The problems of national regulation aren't limited to the UK.

The FT also reported that US Congressmen want the Treasury to insist that banks which have received US funding invest in the US. Reacting to $8 billion of financing that Citi is arranged for public authorities in Dubai and a $7 billion investment by Bank of America in the China Construction Bank, they have raised questions about why US bailout money should be used outside the US.

Several FS Club participants said the FSA liquidity rules, which are to take effect in October, were adding cost to banking without adding much value. Banks will have a difficult time finding some of the data and it is unlikely the FSA will have staff in sufficient numbers, or with sufficient knowledge, to make use of it.

However, some vendors said that the information is more readily available than many banks think. One or two said that banks would actually derive business benefit from following the FSA liquidity regulations because this is information they need.

The new EU regulator and liquidity risk (2009)

The de Larosière Group published a report on EU financial supervision yesterday. The report covers lots of stuff about liquidity risk, regulation and supervision, including the rejection of any need for a single European regulator (ECB won't like that one) and the strengthening of the current key authorities: CEBS, CEIOPS and CESR. These will be renamed the European Banking Authority, the European Insurance Authority and the European Securities Authority, and given new powers including:

- Representation of EU interests with any discussions with non-EU countries.
- Licensing and regulation of any pan-European institutions, such as credit rating agencies and post-trade infrastructures;
- Interpretation authority for any EU legislation with a legal mandate as the final decision-making authority;
- A role as mediator in any disputes between national supervisors;
- An ability to challenge national supervisors' performance; and
- A coordination role during any future crises.

There is also lots of discussion about liquidity risk and it is clear that there is still no definition of how to get liquidity risk management right.

For example, the liquidity section of the report, as discussed on page 18, states that:

> "Measuring and limiting liquidity risk is crucial, but cannot be achieved merely through quantitative criteria ... therefore the assets of the banking system should be examined in terms not only of their levels, but also of their quality (counterparty risk, transparency of complex instruments...) and of their maturity transformation risk (e.g. dependence on short term funding ... (and) the Basel committee should in the future concentrate more on liquidity risk management. Even though this is a very difficult task, it should come forward with a set of norms to complement the existing qualitative criteria (these norms should cover the need to maintain,

given the nature of the risk portfolio, an appropriate mix of long term funding and liquid assets)."

This leads to a logical conclusion and recommendations on page 19:

"**Recommendation 1:** The Group sees the need for a fundamental review of the Basel II rules. The Basel Committee of Banking Supervisors should therefore be invited to urgently amend the rules with a view to:

- Gradually increase minimum capital requirements;
- Reduce pro-cyclicality (boom-bust cycles), by e.g. encouraging dynamic provisioning or capital buffers;
- Introduce stricter rules for off-balance sheet items;
- Tighten norms on liquidity management; and
- Strengthen the rules for bank's internal control and risk management, notably by reinforcing the 'fit and proper' criteria for management and board members.

"Furthermore, it is essential that rules are complemented by more reliance on judgement.

"**Recommendation 2:** In the EU a common definition of regulatory capital should be adopted clarifying whether, and if so which, hybrid instruments should be considered as tier 1 capital. This definition should be confirmed by the Basel Committee."

There's also an amusing 'disclaimer' which states that "the Members of the Group support all the recommendations. However, they do not necessarily agree on all the detailed points made in the report."

I bet!

One year after MiFID, where is liquidity going? (2009)

Fascinating meeting today on liquidity and where it's all going, as I chaired a panel session with Chi-X, Equiduct, Turquoise, NYSE Euronext and Deutsche Bourse. I was amused to find that the LSE was not there, and, instead of LSE, Baikal jumped on stage. Yes, that's Baikal, the LSE's dark pool that will launch in Q3 2009 after being pushed back a quarter due to Lehman Brothers, the partner on the project, collapse.

Anyways, we started with some quiet questions about how things are looking a year after MiFID and what people are seeing.

The first part was a vote from the audience, with the buy side saying that things are far more fragmented and confusing than they ever were, and none of them trading the bulk of their business through the new exchanges.

So liquidity hasn't moved, has it?

Funnily enough, the audience also voted that they would never want to go back to the pre-MiFID world of concentration rules and poor execution, so maybe liquidity will move.

This led to discussions with the panel about their own activities, with several of the new MTFs being asked whether their minimal spread models of business are sustainable in the long-term. In fact, some MTFs are positively discounting and making a loss on every trade. That is unsustainable and several firms said this was bad for the industry.

This led to questions around whether the MTFs were generating more risk in the markets, and whether they could actually manage counterparty risks effectively.

On this point, I raised heckles a little by asking the dumb question: "As EMCF only has two risk managers and is now run by the Dutch government, isn't that bad for business?" Chi-X didn't like that one and refuted it by saying who better to manage counterparty risks than a government?

This led to conversations about new initiatives amongst the incumbent exchanges, with Octopus and Smartpool for NYSE Euronext and Eurex from Deutsche Bourse.

It was interesting that the trend appears to be for traditional incumbents to start diversifying out into new instruments, asset classes and geographies. That's a trend that sounds great in principle, but can be questioned in practice.

As one of the new MTFs contended, "When a firm is losing business to new competition after years in the market, it doesn't make for a very good qualification to branch out and find other stuff to manage, does it?"

We also talked about clearing and settlement, with a clear question arising around the traditional exchanges locking out open clearing borders.

For example, I asked the question direct of Deutsche Bourse, "Why can't I choose to clear through the EuroCCP for Deutsche Bourse executions?" The answer came back stutteringly around something to do with national insolvency laws in Germany.

Yeah, right.

We also talked about dark pools, trading in the most liquid stocks versus mid-caps and small firms, technology and connectivity costs, and much more, with audience questions including a sprinkle of challenging views such as:

- Do you think there is long-term potential for multiple visible venues in the face of ever decreasing charges, or will margins be eroded away to a point where venues can no longer sustain themselves in a profitable manner?
- In the quest for volume and liquidity, MTFs have created very aggressive fee structures, but are these pricing models sustainable?

- How many of the new MTFs are or will be profitable by the end of 2009?
- Do you think there will be more reactions like the Nordic markets, which decided to create their own bank and broker MTF called Burgundy?
- The new MTFs appear to have little capability for price formation, as they all went offline when LSE had tech issues. Are they going to address these areas? And what about the management of counterparty risk?
- Is the lack of exchange interconnectivity hurting the buy side? For example, it's all well and good to create a cost-efficient process for order inception, execution and clearing, but if the cost of connectivity is still high, then it makes no sense.
- What are the incumbents going to do to help reduce clearing and settlement costs?

Finally, at the end of the panel, we got into a rapid-fire discussion of visions of the future, with everyone saying the future would see consolidation of venues. Therefore, we have been through a short period of fragmentation but will see M&A leading to incumbents fighting across borders for liquidity, and the new MTFs jumping leaps and bounds around them.

As one panellist said: "The Federation of European Stock Exchanges currently has around 35 venues; by 2012, two-thirds of those will have been acquired or will disappear as this competitive battle continues."

For me, the result of the conversation was very much a vision of a polarised world where you have large, global trading platforms in multi-asset instruments competing with highly specialised single instrument execution venues that are faster, cheaper, smarter and more automated.

The advantage of the latter is that they are lean and mean, but they are disadvantaged by being limited either in scale, scope, and geography or funding. The former has the advantage of being global and risk concentrators but are disadvantaged by cost, speed and size.

All in all, like most markets, you therefore end up with a couple of gorillas, and then a pack of lions running around them.

Anything in between will get eaten.

Liquidity management ... what's all that about? (2009)

After talking about Wall Street's liquid workers, liquidity risk, liquidity reporting and liquidity management on several occasions, we had a big debate about it in the Financial Services Club a couple of weeks ago.

It interests me because it is such a wide-ranging subject. For example, liquidity in trading is all about having liquid assets to invest or cash. Liquidity in exchanges is all about having volume and market share, while liquidity in payments is all about the management of cash pools.

As a result, any discussion about liquidity tends to draw a wide and diverse crowd, and this meeting was the usual eclectic mix of payments people, technologists and buy and sell side.

The meeting was titled: "This house believes new liquid architectures will dominate strategic plans for 2010", and was chaired by PJ Di Giammarino, who heads up our Capital Markets Chamber.

Panellists included Rick Weinstein, former Head of Global Structured Credit, Dresdner Kleinwort; Andrew Carter, former CRO at Zurich Financial Services and former Head of Group Operational Risk at NatWest; and Don Deloach, CEO of Aleri.

Here's a write-up of the event:

> "The 'huge price tag' involved in the UK Financial Services Authority's (FSA) incoming liquidity regime was a key topic of discussion at last week's Capital Markets Chamber

in London. 'Although senior management is starting to get on board with the changes, operations people have yet to get involved in these projects in most cases,' said PJ Di Giammarino, Chairman of the Chamber.

"There is a considerable lack of understanding about the details of the regulation and its potential impact on the financial services industry. This is gradually changing, however. The very fact that the room was filled to capacity (much like other recent events on the subject) indicates that the industry is starting to take notice of the impending regime changes.

"In order to educate attendees further, Di Giammarino, discussed the main requirements of the new regime, including the new regulatory reports and stress tests that must be introduced. 'The systems and controls requirements will put huge pressure on firms' data systems because of the level of granularity and the speed involved,' he said.

"The panel discussed the potential to spot the next Lehman as a result of these new measures and it was generally agreed that although the regime may help banks to react to risk exposure in a more coordinated manner, it could not prevent another crisis.

"'There's no way this would help a firm to spot the next Lehman. The whole idea of objective, scientific data is a nonsense,' said Rick Weinstein, former head of global structured credit at Dresdner Kleinwort. 'However, it will help you see who your large exposures are to on a global basis.'

"The most controversial aspect of the new regime is the introduction of so-called liquidity buffers, which are due to be introduced in the first half of 2010 during the second implementation phase. 'The idea of a liquidity buffer is a nonsense, the FSA instead needs to ask banks to hold higher capital reserves,' said Weinstein. 'Banks also need to have formal best practice procedures for how to go into liquidation in an orderly fashion.'

"Andrew Carter, former chief risk officer at Zurich Financial Services and member of the Liquidity Risk Action Network (LiRAN), warned attendees that for now they cannot ignore the impact the liquidity risk regime will have and that they must take action now. 'Regulators are going to come down like a tonne of bricks on senior management that do not have an understanding of their liquidity risk exposure,' he said. 'We need to get away from the complacency that is displayed to do with risk information, boards will need to be more engaged and proactive in dealing with the implications of this information.'

"Firms have the option to respond strategically or tactically, added Don Deloach, CEO of risk management system vendor Aleri. 'It would be a shame to miss the opportunity of aggregating this risk data at the atomic level by opting for a purely tactical response', he said. 'Risk management systems can give firms a competitive advantage over other players in the market by allowing them faster speed to react to market events.'

"Around 60% of the audience members indicated that they believe liquidity risk will dominate banks' budgets for next year. The 40% that did not believe it would be the top of the budget list indicated that this was largely due to the confusion still remaining about what exactly the regime will mean for banks' daily practices. 'The fact that the FSA has issued so many consultation papers on the subject has not helped matters,' added one audience member.

"The audience and panellists agreed that the make up of the board is also likely to pose problems with regards to understanding risk. 'Most board members are the top sales people that have been promoted up the ranks of an organisation and not necessarily those that are best placed to understand the business. It also doesn't help that the average term of a CEO is shorter than that of the implementation of a regulation,' said an audience member.

"So, it seems that a lot of problems and challenges are still ahead of the banking industry with regards to getting on board with the FSA's new regime. Although there is a general understanding that tough times are ahead, there is a considerable amount of confusion about the details of the regulation.

"What is certain is that it's going to be costly and the industry can't afford to ignore it."

During the discussions, however, I kept asking myself various questions.

For example, we now talk about global markets needing global solutions and global regulations yet, as demonstrated by the spat between Britain and Brussels, we cannot even agree national and regional regulations, let alone work on global systems and supervisory structures. If we cannot even agree on a competent authority and supervisory structure in a country, who thinks they can get one to work globally?

Similarly, the discussions are around being regulated by a competent authority, but what is a competent authority? The FSA is not a competent authority, so what is? And what is the constituency, profile and structure of staff and management at a competent authority?

Specifically, for real liquidity risk management you need real-time processing, management and reporting. The FSA wants this and the technology to do this exists and has for a while ...

but what's the motivation to spend the cash to achieve this? Investing for risk management is far less conducive historically for a banker, when compared with investing for revenue growth or cost reduction.

And in some ways you could believe that it's good to be too big to fail. If you're too big to fail, you know you'll get bailed out if you do fail. So what does too big to fail do to your attitude towards risk and risk management? There is no risk.

The trouble is that it's all well and good to come up with questions – but what about answers?

My first answer (written in September 2007!) was to have a global data warehouse of data being traded to monitor risk. And the DTCC is finally coming up with an answer on that one, so at least there's a start.

Unfortunately, Europe appears to want its own repository, however, so this debate will rumble on (and on and on) for a long while to come.

Chapter 4 The trading infrastructure: latency, light speed and dark pools

The
Complete
Banker

Introduction

As a result of the rapid evolution of technology, more and more trading is being provided machine-to-machine and server-to-server, rather than funder-to-banker and trader-to-broker. It is the inevitable march of the machines. These machines are now linked globally and enable anyone to execute a trade in under a second globally. It's all networked and fast, and this is game-changing markets as banks and brokers trade billions of messages every day. Is there any limit to the march of the machines? Not really. The only limitation is your imagination.

How fast is fast? Faster than you think! (2010)

One of the excellent presentations delivered at the trading technologies conference I chaired this week was given by Steve Rubinow, EVP and CIO at NYSE Euronext.

Steve talked about how most latency lies in the infrastructure – the "trading ecosystem" as he referred to it – rather than in the applications and the algorithms. This is why there is such a major focus on connectivity, co-location, proximity and ensuring that the latency hand-offs between all the interconnected parts of the ecosystem are minimised.

It is also why I have heard that the exchanges are now charges for rackspace metres. The nearer in the rackspace you want to be to the exchange server, the more the cost. That's a prohibitive game as it always means the most High Frequency Trading (HFT) firms get their orders filled first if they pay the price.

Steve also referenced the regulatory overhead on storage these days, as you have to store every quote, no matter how important or unimportant that quote may be, because it is all part of the trading ecosystem. By way of example, I was chatting with Thomson Reuters recently and heard that they were tracking about 5,000 market movements per second in 2000, a decade ago; today, it's more like 550,000 trade movements – quotes, indications of interest, executions – per second and by the end of the year, they expect this to exceed a million.

Steve corrected me on these numbers by referencing the US Options Exchange, which claims to track 4 million messages per second across the US trading markets, peaking at 10 million per second. Ten million trade movements per second in the US ... that's 60 million trade messages per minute, or almost three billion per day. And they all need to be stored, indexed, referenced and time-stamped.

That got us into a discussion about multithreaded massively parallel processing (MPP) (are you losing the will to live yet?).

As I asked Steve about the recent case of Barclays Capital getting fined by the FSA over their time-stamping on trade flows being out of synch, he made it clear that this is happening a lot because firms built their trading systems in single thread environments – you process everything in sequence – whereas today it's all about processing in multi-thread – you process everything in parallel. That's a core challenge in the systems and applications of the City's trading firms, as it pretty much means re-architecting all systems involved in the pre-trade order management and execution management world built before the mid-2000s. And now we're in a cloud computing world, with trade execution applications moving into widget-based iPhone apps, that's proving a stretch for everyone.

And remember, there's over anything up to 10 million messages per second ... it's all about order flow, efficiency, algorithms and speed.

Steve reckons that, right now, the fastest processing in the world is 250 microseconds.

250 microseconds. How fast is that? 250 microseconds is 0.00025 of a second. 0.00025 of a second. By the time your brain

engaged in reading that last sentence, about three seconds, this would have allowed 12,000 trade movements to have flowed through the systems, or 4,000 per second.

That's today – 4,000 trade movements per second. By the end of the year, Steve reckons that will increase to 10,000 per second (100 microsecond processing) and soon we will get into nanoseconds and picoseconds and femtoseconds.

1.0 second (s) can be broken into:

- 0.001 (a thousandth) millisecond (ms)
- 0.000 001 (a millionth) microsecond (μs)
- 0.000 000 001 (a billionth) nanosecond (ns)
- 0.000 000 000 001 (a trillionth) picosecond (ps)
- 0.000 000 000 000 001 femtosecond (fs)
- 0.000 000 000 000 000 001 attosecond (as)
- 0.000 000 000 000 000 000 001 zeptosecond (zs)
- 0.000 000 000 000 000 000 000 001 yoctosecond (ys)

Jeez, this stuff blows my mind.

Finally, Steve threw in another comment about fraud and security that piqued my interest. He said that "stealing credit card data is child's play; it's where criminals cut their teeth before they go for the big deals", and that NYSE Euronext gets "thousand of potential attack vectors" every day. So they've build a secure system to avoid denial of service, phish, malware and other attacks.

How effective is that system? Very.

Steve presented this anecdote and it's a great story. Last year, there was a massive attack on key US servers through the internet that emanated somewhere in Asia (don't blame the Chinese whatever you do, Steve). Most of the menace was trying to crack into US defence and government systems and the only servers that fell outside that loop were NASDAQ's and NYSE Euronext's.

NYSE Euronext weren't aware of the attack until the Department of Homeland Security rang Steve and said: "do you know you're systems are being cracked?"

That sounded a bit tardy on the CIO's part so, at that point, I thought Steve was about to announce his resignation from the Exchange ... but no, it was because their systems were so secure that the attack had not registered. Steve rang his back office security guys and asked if they were aware of a breakthrough in the system, and they said 'no' because there wasn't one. Their systems designs were so good that they had deflected it.

So he rang the Department of Defence back and said there had been no breakthrough and they were a bit stunned, as most of their systems had been infiltrated through the attack. They asked: "we spend so much on our systems and defences – far more than you – so how come we were compromised and you haven't been."

I think Steve said something like: "that's for me to know and for you to find out ... or pay me to tell you", and put the phone down.

Lovely.

The true power of low latency for Europe's MTFs (2009)

Last Thursday was one of those days where you wake up knowing it's going to be a good one and you go to bed realising that it was … for some that is, but not for everyone.

In my case, I was up with the birds to get into the City and chair a conference all about trading technologies, from smart order routing through low latency equities exchanges and beyond.

On the way into the conference I discovered that for my good friends Peter Randall might not be having his best day as the headlines held the news that he had left Chi-X. This shocked me, as Peter was joining our Financial Services Club's panel on low latency that very evening.

I rang Peter and obviously gave him my best wishes and that I totally understood that he would not be able to join us that evening and wished him well. Then, in the spirit of the City, I immediately grabbed Hirander Misra, COO for Chi-X, and asked if he would take Peter's place that evening, which he did.

Joining Hirander were Todd Golub, COO of NASDAQ OMX and Yann L'Hullier, CIO of Turquoise. Terry Quigley of Colt Telecom and Chris Pickles of BT both joined us as well. Terry and Chris are key advocates and deliverers of low latency networking.

The results were fascinating and, to an extent, staggering. Have a look at this chart from Chi-X.

Speed: Roundtrip Latency By Venue

Chi-X Internal latency is approximately 350 microseconds

Trading Venue	Median Latency (milliseconds)
Chi-X Europe	0.4 (co-located)
Turquoise	< 4
LSE SETS	< 6
NASDAQ OMX Europe	10
Euronext	13
Deutsche Borse Xetra	37
OMX	43
Borsa Italiana	106
SWX	216
SWX Europe	230

Source: Internal system performance measurement statistics for average DMA order messaging in October 2008, supplied by Chi-X trading participant. These internal figures are for round trip latency message acknowledgement based on sending an average number of message to the exchange system and obtaining a response back to the participant's system over the course of a normal day.

These figures are provided for illustrative purposes only and are not intended to represent an independent performance measure of latency.

This is a high-stakes battle where speed is key. Now Chi-X was purposefully stoking up the argument by saying that they could provide a roundtrip order execution in less than 400 microseconds. There are 1,000 microseconds in every millisecond, and a 1,000 milliseconds in every second, so that's fast.

To put it in context, it takes around 400 milliseconds to blink, so Chi-X can process 1,000 back-to-back orders for every time you blink! 1,000 orders every time you blink! I had to write that twice, as it's quite astounding to imagine. That speed may be contingent upon proximity and FIX connections, but even so … 1,000 orders every time you blink!

That means that if it takes you around seven seconds to read this sentence, Chi-X will have processed around 20,000 back-to-back orders, and yet they can process 150,000 messages per second so that's more like 3 million messages processed in those seven seconds. Wow!

So Hirander claimed that Chi-X has the fastest trading system in Europe and scalability to 150,000 messages per second, implying the others did not. The others responded, with Todd saying they could match that volume processing, and Yann making it clear that it's not just about messages but capability.

We then explored more around latency in depth, and how latency is critical if you are smart order routing through the network to these exchanges.

The importance of low latency cannot be stressed enough in the trading room, where it's claimed that a 1-millisecond advantage in trading applications can be worth $100 million a year to a major brokerage firm.

$100 million a year? This is because if you place an order and it misses being filled, it misses being filled. Even if it misses being filled by 1,000,000th of a second, it misses being filled. In other words, you are dead meat. That's the power of latency.

Now, I had a dinner last year with a bunch of folks talking about latency from buy- and sell-side firms, and a few said that latency didn't matter because their internal systems were so messed up that they took minutes to process rather than microseconds.

That's not true, though. If your internal systems are messed up, then sure you're not going to be as effective as an algo trading, smart order routing, co-located broker-dealer with a snazzy execution management system ... but once your orders leave your systems, then they can travel at the same speeds and you should focus on being as fast as the best or, at least, the rest.

This is why some folks are moving their data centres around the globe to maximise latency. I even heard of one bank that found it took 60 milliseconds longer to route orders via New York from London to Tokyo than via Moscow, so they moved their router network hubs to Moscow as a result.

Chris Pickles also made it clear that proximity services – where traders place their order management systems together to reduce speed of processing – alongside co-location services – where traders place their servers into the exchange to minimise latency – impacted where organisations focused their operations.

We then had a lot of dialogue about the differences and differentiation points between Chi-X, Turquoise and NASDAQ OMX, with a few digs here and there. For example, several folks have questioned whether Turquoise can be truly competitive if they are using off-the-shelf systems such as Cinnober's Tradexpress, which has also been selected by the Nordic MTF Burgundy, although they will be on a later release.

Yann L'Hullier retorted that they have changed Cinnober to reflect the London markets operations of Turquoise and processing in the top European stocks so it's not 'vanilla' software.

Equally, there were discussions about measuring and comparing apples with apples, as usual, with leased line, networked or co-located and proximity services all offering different capabilities for processing, as well as differences in FIX FAST and FIX 4.2 and other FIX connections. So it's not all simplicity itself.

Why latency is so important (and Goldman wins) (2010)

Great article in this month's *Bloomberg Markets* magazine on High Frequency Trading (HFT) which, according to Tabb Group, has increased from almost nothing to account for 61% of US stock market activity and 70% of individual trades since 2005. The SEC announced it is to review this area of trading last month but the focus of the article is what this means in reality from a broker dealer view.

Working with Ancero, Bloomberg has compiled a list of the best brokers using their global trade execution prices between July 2008 and June 2009. This is an annual review, and shows the impact of HFT upon the brokerage community, as Goldman Sachs is the clear winner for brokers handling over $25 billion in trades annually.

According to Ancerno, Goldman is the closest at getting orders filled nearest to the price when the order is received, whilst JPMorgan, last year's #1, has fallen to joint fourth with Barclays Capital, behind Bank of America Merrill Lynch and Morgan Stanley.

	The world's best brokers	Loss in basis points
1	Goldman Sachs	-27.5
2	BoA Merrill Lynch	-32.7
3	Morgan Stanley	-33.6
4=	JPMorgan Chase	-34.2
4=	Barclays Capital	-34.2
6	Investment Technology Group (ITG)	-35.6
7	UBS	-36.3
8	Deutsche Bank	-38.8
9	Citigroup	-39.7
10	Credit Suisse	-41.3

A basis point is 0.01%, so Goldman Sachs' 27.5 = 0.275%, or just over quarter of one percent. This means that, for a client who placed an order for 50,000 shares at $10 each with Goldman Sachs, they would get the shares for an average price of $10.275 cents; whilst Bank of America would fill the order at an average price of $10.327 cents; Morgan Stanley at $10.342 cents; and so on.

(Figures represent the difference between the executed stock price and the price when the order was placed for brokerage clients in the four quarters ended on June 30th 2009, according to Ancerno.)

Why has Goldmans won?

According to Roger Freeman, an analyst covering brokerage houses and exchanges at Barclays plc, because "They have the most developed and advanced electronic systems" and "can get some of the fastest execution times on trades."

This is why latency is so critical and illustrates the point well. For example, per day, the US exchanges averaged trading of 10.4 billion shares daily during the year to June 30 2009, with institutional investors globally paying $28.2 billion in trading commissions compared to $30.7 billion in 2008 and $26 billion in 2007.

Interestingly, the basis point difference varies quite widely by region:

Loss in basis points

	USA	Europe	Asia
Goldman Sachs	-25.4	-32.6	-24.0
JPMorgan Chase	-34.1	-35.8	-31.1

This may be a reflection of the early state of low latency in Europe at that time, and demonstrates why Chi-X has succeeded so fast.

Algo and HFT statistics (2010)

I was looking for some stats on HFT and algorithmic trading, and stumbled across a great range of facts and figures on Wikipedia, of all places.

First, we need to just say that HFT and algo trading are different. Algorithmic trading just refers to all and any form of trading using programmed systems that automate the trade cycle. HFT is a more specific area, and uses algo tools to move equities fast. In other words, the holding of stock in an HFT strategy might be for seconds or parts of seconds, whilst algo focuses upon those plus holdings for the medium and long term.

So there is a difference. That's why, when Wikipedia quotes Aite Group as saying that HFT firms account for 73 per cent of all US equity trading volume in 2009, they're wrong. According to Reuters, who should know, high-speed trading "accounts for about 60 percent of US equity volume". Bloomberg agrees, quoting TABB Group which states that HFT accounts for 61% of equities volume, up from 35% in 2007.

There's the key point. HFT is big news, especially when it causes trillion dollar rises and falls.

This is well illustrated when we think about my old forecast that the markets will be run by a man and his dog: the man's there to feed the dog and the dog's there to stop the man touching the keyboard.

Don't think that's true? Back in 2006, 40% of all orders were entered by algo traders at the London Stock Exchange, rising to 60% in 2007 and now estimates believe that around 80% of trading is automated thanks to so many MTFs. Long live the man and his dog!

On that note, I've used this analogy for a long while now but, in researching this stuff again, was surprised to see this conclusion of an interview with yours truly in June 2007:

"As brokers and exchanges scramble to adjust, those who face the biggest risks from algorithmic trading may very possibly be small-scale investors – those most reliant on market stability, good governance and fair access to information and technology.

"'Many of the algorithmic trading strategies include risk strategies untested by market downturns,' warns Balatro's Chris Skinner. 'A lot of the traditional market stabilizers are being taken out' by the trading speed and fluidity enabled by algorithmic trading, he adds.

"The biggest stabiliser of all, he notes, is perhaps the role of local and national financial regulators. "But in the new era of algorithmic trading, in which trading technologies and strategies are closely-held competitive secrets fiercely protected from scrutiny, Skinner says regulators will have a tough time gaining sufficient information to 'understand what they are regulating.' Especially if it's happening in 10 or 20 jurisdictions simultaneously. It all starts to make Enron's famously complex trading strategies look simple, he adds.

"After all, Skinner notes, if major Canadian banks find it necessary to outsource their algorithmic trading expertise because it's too expensive to go it alone, how likely is it that our notoriously parsimonious financial regulators – with their laughably small technology budgets – will be able to ensure the world's increasingly fleet-footed algo-experts always play fair?"

How prophetic?

High frequency trading in jeopardy thanks to flash crash (2010)

No-one could have missed the markets flash drop in May.

On 6th May, US markets fell into a trillion dollar freefall. Accenture's shares fell from $41 at 2:30 that afternoon to just one cent each by 2:47 whilst Apple's shares soared 40,000 per cent to reach $100,000 each during the same 20- minute period. Overall, the US stock market lost 9 per cent of value before rebounding just as fast. The result is that the SEC is bringing in rules that will stop a freefall by freezing any equity whose price moves more than 10 per cent in any five-minute period. This may deal with the issue but does it deal with the cause?

For over a decade electronic trading has progressed from simple puts and calls to hugely complex structures. A decade ago, FIX Protocol was designed to streamline connectivity between buy and sell side, whilst today it is designed to allow millions of trade offers of indications of interest and order cancellations to take place in real-time, low latency operations.

This point was brought home to me in conversation with Thomson Reuters in the UK, who tell me that, in 2000, they were following 5,000 trading changes per second. This figure had increased to 550,000 changes per second today, and the exchanges expect this to reach over a million by the end of year. In New York, the figures are 10 times this level, with the US Options Exchange claiming to track four million messages per second across the US trading markets, peaking at 10 million per second.

Algorithmic black box structures have stretched the point further, by moving from simple trading of stocks to complex trading strategies that seek arbitrage opportunities at every point of the trade lifecycle. For example, these complex layers of trading strategies have allowed the rise of cross-asset class trading, where a simple trade call for Microsoft stock can be hedged with a link to other tech stocks, such as Apple and IBM, mixed with FX pricing movements and the speed of rises and falls on the Dow and S&P 500, all in real-time. This is why we find the interlinkage and complexities of trading created by such technologies are rapidly becoming more precarious.

A point that was obvious to me back in August 2007 when Goldman Sachs' systems messed up losing 30 percent of the value, or $1.5 billion, of their flagship global equity funds in a week. Goldmans' CFO David Viniar said that this was because they were "seeing things that were 25-standard deviation events, several days in a row." A 25-standard deviation event is meant to only happen once every 100,000 years.

It was obvious that systems seeking arbitrage opportunities could get their models wrong and, since the implosion of liquidity in 2008 when Lehman Brothers failed, we know how fragile these systems can be.

It has not stopped the ongoing march of investment innovation however, with the latest sprinkling of low latency for high frequency trading added to the melting pot. For example, the CIO of NYSE Euronext said to me recently that the fastest processing in the investment world processes in about 250 microseconds today, or 0.00025 of a second. In other words, in the time it took you to read the last sentence, about 10 seconds, about 40,000 trade movements could have flowed sequentially through the system.

And all of those trades movements need to be time stamped, recorded and indexed for client and regulatory reporting purposes, which is why firms ranging from Barclays to Instinet to Credit Suisse have all received fines from the FSA recently for incorrect time reporting of trades.

And every nanosecond is the difference between getting the trade executed or losing the trade execution opportunity to a competitor. So this march of high frequency complex arbitrage-based automated trading will continue. Unless regulators stop it, that is.

The fact is that the SEC and FSA in the USA and UK respectively are really concerned about such developments, particularly with the issues created by 'flash orders', where a sell side firm might change prices in real-time between a client's order and its execution in order to make a buck at their expense.

Similarly, regulators are fearful of things they do not understand or hear stories about that sound like in appropriate use of information systems, such as 'dark pools'. Dark pools, where orders are placed unseen by the lit markets, are actually good for liquidity according to institutional investors and trading institutions, but have an issue just due to their title: 'dark'.

Dark is scary and that's why rumours of the new European revision of the Markets in Financial Instruments Directive might crack down on dark pool trading structures and worse.

All in all, we are living through a moment in time where the steady march of technology to create innovative trading opportunities are likely to be reined in by regulatory authorities who fear irrational and unexpected market movements in real-time.

The question is: how much of a brake can they put on such innovation? My answer would be: not much. After all, most regulations result in unexpected consequences, e.g. MiFID moved a third of all European equities trading from traditional exchanges to high frequency automated trading pools. Do they really want to reverse this trend?

I don't think so. So it's all about checks and balances ... or is that cheques and bank balances?

Flash Goldman (2009)

I had a chat with a couple of people last week about the hot topics in capital markets. Along with our regular talk about liquidity risk, new EU regulations and USA and EU focus upon OTC derivatives, clearing and settlement, another subject has recently come to the fore.

The use of broker-dealer capabilities to leverage latency and electronic liquidity to gain a buck at the expense of the buy side, better known as 'flash trading'.

This has become a hot topic, because the regulators recently learnt that this can cause issues, especially when we're talking about dark pools where large block order trades can be executed with zero visibility to the wider markets.

It's also been a focus of conversation for a while. For example, at TradeTech in April we talked about 'gaming' using the buyer's key indicators of trading activity electronically. These are based upon two messages: an Indication of Interest (IOI) and Immediate or Cancel Order (IOC); and these are the source of concern within the industry.

> "The misuse of IOIs and IOCs is a hot debate topic, as many dark pools use this information badly to allow leakage and hence 'gaming'. For example, you receive 16 orders for 62,500 IBM shares from one fund manager or broker dealer and you know that a million shares are moving, probably on the basis of news or views of one player.
>
> "Using IOIs and IOCs, other traders can then game those IBM shares, moving prices using dark pools. Then combine IOIs and IOCs with latency arbitrage and you can see how complicated this all gets."

Before we get too complicated, it is probably best to explain some of the lingo used here.

The IOI is the buyer's message saying that they might want to place an order for so many shares in a stock and the IOC is used to cancel the order.

In the case of flash trading, the high speed processing means that some brokers can use systems to see a trade coming into the market, and raise the price artificially by processing a series of other buy requests before the order is executed.

In other words, the combination of high frequency trading using super-fast, low latency systems that are highly automated, allow the market making firms to use a 'flash' order which is visible for let's say half a second, to make a few dollars.

Half a second is 500 milliseconds or 500,000 microseconds (there are 1,000 milliseconds in 1 second; 1000 microseconds in 1 millisecond; and so on) which is why speed is so important, and the automated market-making firms with naked access can use a flash order to advantage for this reason.

But it's not just low latency. It's the use of technology, algorithmic trading, co-location and proximity-hosted, high frequency, low value trading, combined with low latency that makes this all so darned complicated ... and the more complicated, the more likely and capable are those who understand the markets able to make a buck.

That's why Goldman Sachs was so worried when it lost one of its programmers, and potentially its program code, last month. This has now raised the regulatory radar, with the US the first to crack down.

According to several reports last week, the SEC is making moves to ban flash trades, and NASDAQ and BATS are also moving to block flash trades.

That's all well and good. However, all exchanges are struggling to find volume and liquidity right now and just as some may introduce restrictive practices, others – such as Euronext – build new capabilities to incentivise high frequency traders and trading.

Result: there will be more moves to restrict this type of trading using regulatory restraints.

Result + 1: the market makers and exchanges will create even more convoluted technologies and program trading capabilities to evade these restraints.

And so the cycle goes ...

Lower latency in the trading room (2009)

A good day all in all, with lots of discussion about technologies in the trading room, latency and related matters.

My favourite presentation was from the new CEO of Chi-X, Mark Howarth, who outlined their success in the last few months. Earlier in the day, we had a panel comprising Larry Tabb, CEO of TABB Group; Donal Byrne, CEO of Crovil; and Stephane Leroy, Head of Global Sales & Marketing at the Quant House.

The focus of the discussion was latency and what it means, but we went around a whole range of subjects from direct market access to smart order routing, dark pools to algorithmic trading, MTFs to new quant houses (and not Stephane's) ... the dialogue focused upon new business models, redefining old ways of doing business and the future ways of trading.

Future trading comes down to cost, transparency and speed, and doing things in another way. Doing things in another way means melding the quantitative analytics with the technology in real-time, and that's what low latency comes down to. This builds upon the general discussion about latency here, but adds the key new dimension of latency arbitrage.

This is the key: if you can find a deal a micro or milli or nano second earlier than another dealer, then you've made a gain because you sell that deal a micro or milli or nano second earlier and make a buck, or many bucks.

There's the rub, because firms are seeking a latency delta, so it's not the latency but the latency lag and arbitrage that makes the difference.

Meantime, all the talk of OMS, EMS, DMA, Algo, MTFs, multi-asset and more (go figure?) is just talk, because it all comes down to the fusion of the human with the technology to create arbitrage opportunities.

The real-time integration of the man-machine is the true vision of future trading markets and whether you're a broken model of business, an emerging star or a key long-term player, as long as you can deal in real-time with intelligence then you can make money in these markets.

Even now.

Lesson learned, and more to come.

SEC to crack down on HFT? (2010)

I often return to the theme of latency and high frequency trading (HFT). So a friend tipped me to look at the SEC's latest consultation document released in January on trading in American equities markets. Interesting section at the bottom of page 62:

"Latency of Consolidated Data

The Commission requests comment on all aspects of the latency between consolidated data feeds and individual trading center data feeds.

What have market participants experienced in terms of the degree of latency between trading center and consolidated data?

Is the latency as small as possible given the necessity of the consolidation function, or could plan processor systems be improved to significantly reduce the latency from current levels, while still retaining the high level of reliability required of plan processors?

More broadly, is the existence of any latency, or the disparity in information transmitted, fair to investors or other market participants that rely on the consolidated market data feeds and do not use individual trading center data feeds?

If so, should the unfairness be addressed by a requirement that trading center data be delayed for a sufficient period of time to assure that consolidated data reaches users first?

Would such a mandated delay adequately address unfairness?

Would a mandatory delay seriously detract from the efficiency of trading and harm long-term investors and market quality?

Should the Commission require that additional information be included in the consolidated market data feeds?"

I think change is afoot ... and will MiFID Wave 2 do the same?

Payments in the trading room and investment markets (2009)

In the securities settlement markets, we've spent years trying to break down barriers to clearing and settlement ... and most of those barriers are still there.

We wonder what to do about it. And regulation seems the only answer. Or is it? Let's look at payments in the trading room and investment markets. There are clearly some things afoot which will change things.

The first is that everything is real-time or supra real-time. Sure, we talk about fast and scalable systems, but in the trading arena we're talking not just fast but super-fast. (...) This is the world of latency, which really does bring in a new focus on real-time.

(...)

Now think about liquidity, risk, clearing and settlement and imagine a world where, as you trade:

- Your complete picture of liquidity positions are transparent to all traders internally;

- Your liquidity risk exposures, market and credit risk exposures and more are visible to all counterparties in real-time.;
- Your trade reporting and pricing is visible to all regulatory and supervisory authorities in real-time;
- And real-time clearing takes place as part of trade execution.

This world is not a future vision but a reality.

Eurex, for example, thanks to being tightly coupled with a clearing system (Eurex Clearing), are already offering real-time clearing.

Meanwhile, we have regulators moving further and further towards information reporting duties that go far beyond today's methods.

That is why real-time trade and risk reporting will be a reality in the near-term. End-of-day just doesn't cut it. Intra-day doesn't manage it. Real-time everything.

That's the future of investment markets. Real-time visibility and transparency for all counterparties to manage risk.

Mmmm ... now it gets interesting.

Look deep into my dark pools (2009)

It's a line I've wanted to use in conversation for a long-time but never found the opportunity and now here it is: "look deep into my dark pools".

No, I haven't made a mess or done something socially unacceptable. I'm just looking at the latest trading phenomena where buyers can place large trades into a market exchange and they sit there until sellers offer a good enough price for the volume.

Ker-ching, trade executes. It works the same vice-versa and is well illustrated by Turquoise's "How it Works" page.

Some people believe that the dark pool is a worryingly new phenomenon, but it is not. As Chair of the TradeTech discussions, Andrew Silverman, Managing Director for Electronic Trading with Morgan Stanley, stated in a story about when he first joined the investment markets back in the 1980s.

Then, the head of the trading floor would receive a large block order that needed trading in the dark and so he would split the order.

So let's say a large buy-side firm wants to trade a million IBM shares. The order would be separated into two orders of 500,000 shares each across two of the firm's trading desks. The head of those desks would allocate 250,000 shares to the lead technology traders in their team. Quite often those traders would then split the trade further to two of their technology analysts, who might then split the deal again to the junior traders recently joining the firm, such as Andrew back in those heady days.

Andrew would trade 62,500 IBM shares and have no idea that he and the other 15 traders were all dealing at the same time on behalf of the same client for a total order of a million IBM shares. In other words, on ly 62,500 shares in this trade are 'lit' whilst 937,500 shares were in the 'dark'.

So dark has been with us a long time. It's just that today, it's a lot faster.

As Andrew stated when he opened the discussion: "I can remember in 1982 latency was three minutes. Now, it is a millionth of a second and getting faster."

My, how far we've come and soon ... real-time dark trading in a perfect market? Not quite yet, but we're not far off.

To discuss such matters, Andrew introduced a panel comprising:

- Yvette Roozenbeek, Executive Director, Strategic Development, NYSE Euronext for SmartPool;

- Robert Boardman, Head of Algorithmic Trading, ITG; and
- Daniel Keegan, Global Head of Electronic Execution Sales, Citi.

Various comments and quotes popped out of the woodwork. For example, "it's where you sit in the dark pool queue that is critical".

Too right. With today's low latency systems if you're not at the front of queue and other block orders are there ahead of you, you might be sitting for a while before any of the order is filled for your block trades.

To be honest, it isn't supposed to work that way as, under best execution rules, dealers are meant to process orders in the sequence they arrive. However, with dark orders, this is not necessarily the case as a dark order can sit on the books for as long as it takes to be filled, whilst other orders pass through.

One panellist commented: "Although a dark order is filled, you have to ask where the price comes from. The price is not in the dark, but the order fill can be from a price that is not of the moment because size is discovered in the dark whilst price is public."

Sounds like some form of bedroom discussion, but it is much more to do with the dark orders being for large trading volumes of low frequency, where keeping a player's hand close to their chest is key.

This means that dark pools are there to offer a method of trading where orders are not based upon the visible market price but on mid-point matching, for example. Now mid-point matching – the difference between Bid and Offer – may be OK, but in a world of Best Bid-Offer, Best Execution and pre-trade transparency, this seems to fly a little in the face of MiFID's aims.

Another panellist pointed out that: "Although you may have the legal right to ask brokers where they trade and with which execution venues, the fact that the European press are different is the reason why pre-trade is so hard to deal with."

This seemed to be getting at the idea that you may have pre-trade rules in the US and Europe that strive to be the same ... but that the European press is always looking for news and rumours, and hence will stir up market stories that may not even be true based upon access to full price transparency and visibility.

Citi's Dan Keegan then jumped in with a comment that about 30 percent of Citi's trading book is dark but that the numbers vary dependent upon how you define "off of primary". This is based upon the fact that you have three books of business:

1. A light book of business, which is visible to the markets for price discovery;
2. A grey book of business, which has some lit areas such as price, and some dark areas such as block order trading volumes; and
3. A dark book of business, which is invisible to the open market place (the primary market) in both price and size.

The whole point of this is that there is always a danger of information leakage, where transparency of trading, especially block order trading of size, can be leaked for both insider and press analysis.

That's the whole point of dark – to trade with the other investors being unaware of how and what you are trading, particularly if you are a market maker or market mover and shaker.

And, sorry to get into such detail but it is important, this brings in other areas of the trade order cycle, namely two pieces of information: Indication of Interest (IOI) and Immediate or Cancel Order (IOC).

IOI is an invitation to see if anyone can trade an order you are thinking about placing, and IOC moves markets as it uses IOIs to trade and then immediately negates the trade before it is filled.

Using such information allows traders, if they see a market mover trading, to buck the price without ever placing an order. This is why it is so important to keep IOIs and IOCs secret, especially in dark pools where major players are placing high value orders in low volumes.

In fact, the misuse of IOIs and IOCs is a hot debate topic, as many dark pools use this information badly to allow leakage and hence 'gaming'.

For example, you receive 16 orders for 62,500 IBM shares from one fund manager or broker dealer and you know that a million shares are moving, probably on the basis of news or views of one player.

Using IOIs and IOCs, other traders can then game those IBM shares, moving prices using dark pools. Then combine IOIs and IOCs with latency arbitrage and you can see how complicated this all gets.

For example, the US markets have about 45 dark pools and managing the complexity of all that liquidity across so many venues is proving incredibly difficult, as well as providing lots of opportunities for gaming.

Lots more chat about such stuff and, at the end of it, a question around how to deal with such pools and regulate them, if at all.

The answer? It's a trade-off between innovation and transparency, and you cannot have full transparency if it is at the expense of market innovation.

I'm not sure I concur with this point, as many say that our markets are in the mess they are in today thanks to innovation.

In fact, it's interesting that if you combine the points made by others about avoiding regulation at the expense of innovation, you do wonder what all of this means. I think it means something around the themes raised by Anthony Hilton, City Editor of the *Evening Standard* yesterday:

> "Trade unions could not believe it when 30 years ago prime minister Margaret Thatcher said she would no longer listen to them, give them privileges or allow them a special place in the economic order.
>
> "They had become so used to flexing their economic muscle and being listened to by government that they came to believe their own publicity. They thought they were so special, so irreplaceable, so essential to the functioning of the economy that no one would dare to try to run things without them. They seemed genuinely to believe they had a divine right to a disproportionate share of the country's economic output.
>
> "It took a long time for them to realise the world had moved on, and the mass of the public had switched off. Their behavioural excesses had destroyed their mystique and provoked a backlash so severe that most of us were no longer interested in them or their ideas – still less their prosperity.
>
> "Today's senior bankers have a lot in common with those unions. They too have spent a decade over-exploiting their economic and political muscle, straying well beyond their original purpose, pretending to a mystique and importance they do not possess and trying to extract unjustifiably large rewards for their labours. They too have ultimately been brought down by their arrogance.
>
> "And they still don't seem to get it."

In other words, like bank bonuses and OTC credit derivatives, I have a strong feeling that anything which creates additional risks in the future by being dark may become noticed by policymakers as unacceptable risk and lit-up.

Shame.

Integrated investing in a connected world (2008)

After picking holes in banking infrastructures, and the lack of integration the institutions have with today's connected world, there is one part of the market that really gets technology. They do not just get technology, but they lead in it. Where? Investment markets. The investment markets are more than just connected with the world of technology today. They are integrated with it.

You only have to look at the exchanges, like the refreshed London Stock Exchange (LSE) and upstart Chi-X, to hear of trade processing taking place at the speed of light. An order on these exchanges can be processed faster than the blink of an eye, and the order flows are all managed through an agreed pre-trade standard, FIX.

This does not mean that it is all tickety-boo in the investment garden of roses, as there are many flavours of FIX (4.0, 4.1, 4.2, 4.3, 4.4, 5.0 ...) and order routing does not always go to the best trading platforms (you would not need RegNMS if this were true), but the investment markets are a hotbed of technology leadership in banking.

Take the latest algorithmic platforms. Gone are the days of simple black box algo trading, when a trading strategy might be something along the lines of 'when A goes up and B goes down, then buy lots of B whilst selling lots of A.' This simplicity just does not work anymore.

Today's automated trading strategies are more like: 'when A goes up and B goes down on NASDAQ, and C's Volume Weighted Average Price (VWAP) moves by more than 0.15% within a 30 minutes period on NYSE, then buy B and C whilst taking out a forward option on A.' Throw in a few currency hedges and a government bond and you get the idea.

It has moved from simple open outcry, or shouting at each other, to complex cross-asset global automated hedged trading. And it all takes place at light speed.

This is why traders use scenario modelling and quant analytics to play out trading strategies offline before playing out these strategies in real-time. This is why buy-side firms are rolling out massively complex smart order routing systems in order to build straight-through processing capabilities. This is why broker-dealers have been buying up execution management system providers in order to offer integrated end-to-end infrastructures.

Today's investment markets are all about speed and latency in order to gain an arbitrage buck ahead of the pack.

Take the business of exchanges. Massively complex algorithmics combined with globally connected order management systems have changed the whole nature of deal volumes and trading strategies. For example, Deutsche Bourse announced their quarterly earnings this week, showing that their cash equities platform, Xetra, enjoyed a 4% rise in trading volumes through the first quarter of this year over the same quarter last year.

Not bad. But then their derivatives platform, Eurex, enjoyed a 52% rise in volumes during the same period, contributing 42% of earnings compared to 17% from Xetra.

NYSE Euronext and other exchanges are showing similar trends.

This demonstrates that we no longer deal in a world of stocks and shares, but we deal with a world of fractions of future equities and commodities tied to hedged FX and underlying instruments.

It is this ability to build more and more complex futures trading strategies, using complex systems analytics to deal in higher volumes at lower values that separates the winners from the losers.

It is enabling firms to split block trades and deliver highly integrated trading strategies anonymously into the markets. It is the enabling of these markets through the speed and complexity of today's massively parallel, virtualised, grid- and cloud-based systems, that allows these firms to hedge, arbitrage, manage risk and leverage across global markets, and gain advantage over the chasing pack.

The speed, complexity and structure of global investment markets may demonstrate some of the connections we will need to build into payments and banking infrastructures generally in the future.

For example, one broker-dealer recently changed their whole infrastructure to gain an extra 60 milliseconds of speed. To get that 60 milliseconds, they moved their server farm from New York to Moscow. The reason is that, for every 100 kilometres of cabling, a delay of up to one millisecond is added to the speed of processing. By moving processing to Moscow, this broker can therefore trade from London to Tokyo in 180 milliseconds, rather than 240 milliseconds via New York.

This is the future of banking. Creating infrastructures that deliver not just faster payments and global connections, but instant connections through global infrastructures.

The challenge then is how to manage risks effectively when you can shift millions or even billions of dollars in the blink of an eye.

- How do we manage fraud in these future environments?
- How do you ensure data integrity?
- As you press that button, did you really mean to buy that stock, move that money, make that assertion, deal with that trader?

After all, in this globally connected world of light speed technologies, you cannot take anything back. Once the button is pressed, you have done the deal, made the transaction, processed the order, agreed the contract.

What an interesting world we live in.

Chapter 5 New trading venues and incumbent exchanges

Introduction

Thanks to the march of the machines, new and more efficient trading platforms have been launched. These platforms are taking liquidity from traditional exchanges because they offer super-efficient processing at a fraction of the cost of the incumbents. For example, Europe's new trading platforms process for about a tenth of the cost or less of the traditional exchanges. Result: after less than three years, one in five trades had moved from old and inefficient exchanges to new ones. That's 20% of the total market for trading, and it's growing fast. The game has changed.

MTFs versus incumbent exchanges, Round 1 (2009)

There were two great discussions during TradeTech that compared and contrasted the incumbents with the new MTFs (Multilateral Trading Facilities) created by MiFID. The first focused upon attracting liquidity and what that means; the second on the likely view for the future of trading venues.

The first discussion was a debate chaired by Andrew Silverman, Managing Director, Electronic Trading, Morgan Stanley, amongst a panel comprising:

- Hirander Misra, COO, Chi-X Europe;
- John Wilson, Chief Executive, Baikal;
- Rainer Riess, Managing Director, Cash Market Business Development, Deutsche Bourse;
- Mark Hemsley, CEO, BATS Trading Europe; and
- Simon Brickles, CEO, Plus Markets Group.

There was a little of the usual spikey stuff about "our exchange is better/cheaper/ faster than yours," especially when Hirander of Chi-X mentioned how their order execution was 1.6 basis points better than Xetra's, to which Rainer of Deutsche Bourse responded that: "Chi-X can claim a 1.6 bps improvement over

Xetra, but Xetra could claim a 10 bps improvement over Chi-X dependent upon how you measure it."

Herr Riess was quite fired up, in fact, and continued: "You must not confuse reality with marketing. It reminds me of the bargain airlines, for example, where you advertise very cheap seats but when you try to book, the seats are not there. Ignoring the depth of book is not useful."

Ah yes, the old apples and pears difficulties of comparing the full execution, clearing and settlement cycle, although there has to be some truth in Hirander's claims or why would Chi-X have picked up so much market share off the incumbents over the last two years?

There were also some key notes of substance during this panel as well, such as Rainer's closing comment that you cannot ignore the depth of the book when comparing execution venues.

Mark Hemsley counteracted that liquidity flows to BATS because they have "tighter prices, a diversified customers base and no dependence upon a single order flow"; whilst Hirander talked the fact that regulations mandate Best Bid-Offer (BBO) reference pricing which, without a consolidated tape for a European BBO-(EBBO) style service – which Equiduct offers if anyone's interested – then you cannot achieve this BBO capability.

Equally, Hirander stated that you need EBBO with Volume Weighted Average Pricing (VWAP) to make it really work. True. John Wilson agreed, but clarified that a mandated tape would be a bad thing because it would create latency issues and challenges in determining where to take the prices from.

In fact, the entire panel felt a consolidated reference pricing on a single tape would be great, but that is should not be a regulatory requirement. Morgan Stanley's Andrew Silverman then made the most telling comment: "Fix it or we will be regulated".

Also true.

There was also a clear view that the clearing and settlement area is a problem, with Mark Hemsley of BATS saying it was "a joke" due the log-jam of requests for change. "We will go out of our way to support those clearers who create interoperability", and that there was room for three pan-European CCPs maximum.

John Wilson of Baikal agreed, saying that interoperability of CCPs is critical which is why CCP intermediation is increasing. With intermediation increasing, CCPs are now concerned about disintermediation, which is why interoperability and risk models are being opened up for discussion between the Clearing and Settlement Mechanisms (CSMs).

Implication: EuroCCP and EMCF are going to get the full support to lean on Eurex Clearing and Euroclear to make change happen.

Rainer Riess then countered with a view that the Code of Conduct had created transparency and debate, and that there is competition so we do not need more regulation. Equally, in the clearing space, you have to remember the issues of risk and that interoperability between two CCPs are hard to control. "An integrated vertical silo is needed, and we can do that in that we can marginalise across asset classes." Rainer finished with the view that you "must balance competition against market integrity".

Implication: Deutsche Bourse with Xetra, Eurex and Eurex Clearing has the straight-through processing under a single umbrella for end-to-end trading clearing and settlement ... if you want to avoid risk and / or prefer a more single provider (competitors call 'monopoly') approach.

All in all, a great panel session.

MTFs versus incumbent exchanges, Round 2 (2009)

Andrew Silverman, Managing Director, Electronic Trading for Morgan Stanley, chaired the second day's sessions at TradeTech with a great dialogue about attracting liquidity between the new exchanges, the MTFs and the incumbents.

This led to a second discussion of the future of trading venues with panel members:

- Cees Vermaas, Executive Director, Sales and Relationship Management, NYSE Euronext and NYSE ARCA EUROPE MTF;
- Hugh Brown, Head of Secondary Markets Product Development, London Stock Exchange (LSE) Group;
- Eli Lederman, CEO, Turquoise;
- Charlotte Crosswell, President, NASDAQ OMX Europe; and
- Artur Fischer, Joint CEO, Equiduct Trading.

Here's my summary notes.

The Chair kicked off the dialogue by asking Eli if the new MTFs could really attack Europe's major markets when they are only cash equities players. Eli responded by saying that the focus of MiFID's intentions is to create transparency and visibility in the cash equities markets, and there will be a view that this needs to move into other asset classes, especially derivatives.

However, the focus today is still on cash equities as the job there is still only just starting. This means creating an order flow that allows a greatly increased flow of smaller orders at higher volumes alongside dark book business for larger orders at lower frequencies.

The Chair then stepped in and stated that no-one only trades just equities, casting doubt on the MTFs' ability to attract liquidity as a solo asset class player. He then moved to Charlotte Crosswell of NASDAQ OMX Europe and asked why they weren't amalgamating OMX Nordic into NASDAQ OMX.

Charlotte responded by saying that they didn't "want to cannibalise our own markets, but we do need to be pan-European. So yes, we do compete with ourselves between OMX and NASDAQ to provide choices. We just don't advertise if one is doing better than the other in the Nordic region."

The discussion then moved into the increasing competitiveness of broker-dealers who, with their own dark pools and low latency platforms, are increasingly competing direct with the incumbents anyway. Hedge funds become market markets and brokers become exchanges, all mean that the clarity and division of the markets is blurring and clouding over.

At this point, it was interesting that Charlotte raised a concern of the new players. "We are the cheapest venue out there on Best Bid-Offer (BBO) but we are not getting the volume ... smart order routing is not right yet and so we keep adjusting our pricing. It all comes down to the post-trade issues, however, as execution costs have come down to a minimum. We can all compete at 0.1 basis points or thereabouts, but order routers ignore that because of the elephant in the room, namely clearing and settlement."

I liked that comment, as many of our CCPs and CSDs are a bit elephant-like, e.g. slow to change. And how do you eat an elephant? One piece at a time. We will get there, and EMCF and EuroCCP are just the start.

We also discussed the maker-taker model, where some players provide liquidity whilst others take it. Right now, the MTFs charge a higher basis point for taking liquidity, but they are experimenting with their models between the maker-taker model versus a flat rate of, let's say, 0.01 bps for each trade. This hybrid structure is likely to grow.

The Chair then asked whether such short-term price promotions only encourage short-term liquidity, and long-term is still with the incumbents.

Hugh Brown of LSE liked that point, and stated the pricing only ever has a one-way direction, and that is downwards. He then noted that the new MTFs are not profitable yet and, with pricing unsustainable today and even more likely to be squeezed tomorrow, felt that their long-term viability and sustainability was questionable.

Artus Fisher of Equiduct agreed, saying that "we made a mistake to get into a price war". The fact that the new MTFs have a low cost base, hi-tech platform with low latency, minimal fixed costs and more, should be the advantages they trade with rather than an unsustainably low-cost promotion which means we cannot survive.

All in all, an interesting chat about the future of the markets which was inconclusive. The fact is that you have one big new disruptive MTF, Chi-X, which gained first-mover advantage. The others are challenged.

For example, when asked 'What is the one thing you would change?', Charlotte Crosswell piped up: "Not launching in September 2008" and quite rightly pointed out that when the MTFs were laying the launch plans, none of them could foresee the long-haul of liquidity drought we were going to suffer after Lehman Brothers collapse.

Therefore, Chi-X is a survivor – and the others? Without strong backing with deep pockets for a three-year cycle of deep discounted promotions and liquidity challenges based upon price improvement not being the only battlefront, several may not survive.

I wrote an in-depth review of this area for Colt Telecom during the fall of 2008, which may provide some useful background. Although the landscape has changed since then, my conclusions are the same, which is that there's only room for three MTFs of any note.

Order routers not providing best execution (2009)

Chi-X began trading two years ago, soon to be followed by Turquoise, BATS, NASDAQ OMX and Equiduct. And there will be more. According to the dialogue so far, there are 125 or so MTFs registered with CESR across Europe.

Admittedly, many of these are broker-dealer based systems and services, but there are at least 10 pan-European MTFs registered, with Burgundy the next to launch.

So it's obvious that not all of them can succeed, but having three or four in each area of service from dark pools to liquid stocks to all markets, and eventually to derivatives, bonds, fixed income and other markets, certainly seems to be on the cards according to the discussions here so far.

Right now Chi-X is the one that shouts loudest, probably because it's been around for longest and has first-mover advantage. In fact, unlike BATS, NASDAQ OMX and Equiduct, it also had the advantage of launching well before September 2008 when the credit crisis hit, which is a definite advantage.

Gross consideration for Chi-X rose steadily through to September 2008 and then dipped away as follows:

Gross consideration (€bn)

Q2	07	€1.5
Q3	07	€20.2
Q4	07	€34.6
Q1	08	€74.2
Q2	08	€132.5
Q3	08	€246.3
Q4	08	€205.5
Q1	09	€148.9

Now you may look at those numbers diving since Q3 2008 and think Chi-X should be worried, but that's not the whole story in that, by the end of Q1 2009, Chi-X proudly claim fifth spot in the European pecking order of exchanges, closely followed by NASDAQ OMX Nordic and Turquoise:

Value of equity trading, March 2009

Exchange/MTF	Order book trades	Order book T/over(€m)
1 London Stock Exchange	17,279,867	123,650.0
2 Euronext	15,365,479	116,839.0
3 Deutsche Bourse	8,118,311	95,835.8
4 Spanish Exchange (BME)	2,832,093	60,682.8
5 Chi-X Europe	10,554,888	57,168.5
6 Borsa Italiana	6,227,802	45,937.2
7 SWX Europe	2,875,388	45,495.4
8 NASDAQ OMX Nordic	4,802,676	43,150.6
9 Turquoise	3,309,508	22,567.8
10 Oslo Bors	1,240,279	11,397.7
11 BATS Europe	1,760,985	8,277.7
12 SIX Swiss Exchange	462,090	2,802.3

Equally, market share of all the new exchanges has been steadily rising. For example, the three new MTFs – Chi-X, BATS and Turquoise – are averaging around 20% of the DAX30 daily volume. That's a wee dent in the Deutsche Bourse's pie, I suspect.

In fact, Chi-X's research shows that there would be a significant shift in liquidity and market share to Chi-X and the other MTFs from the incumbent exchanges if best price routing were in play. This would be in the order of 17% of all orders for November 2008, 15% in December, 13% in January 2009 and 12% in February. The reason for the decreasing numbers is the decreased volume of trading during these months, rather than any uncompetitive aspects of the new MTF models.

In other words, and I've heard this from the other MTFs too, the fact that order routers aren't smart enough to seek out best price in Europe right now is the reason why the liquidity sticks with the incumbents.

Not sure if true, but Chi-X claims its market share would have been 10.6% higher between November and February if the full price improvement transparency and best execution rules were enforced.

Old boys versus the new boyz (2010)

I've just been at another fascinating conference on trading and low latency in the capital markets. I thought you might be interested in these stats from Karel Lanoo, CEO of CEPS (not exceptions processing – the Council of European Policy Studies).

He compared the London Stock Exchange's trading and volumes before and after MiFID. Here's the numbers:

		Trades (m)	Turnover (€bn)
On order book (electronic)	2006	78.2	€2.2
	2009	156.4	€1.27
Off order book (OTC)	2006	16.5	€3.77
	2009	9.63	€1.28

And you may think that's down to the fact that the LSE has been hit by lower volume of trading thanks to the crisis. Yes, in part:

	Trades (m)	Turnover (€bn)
2008	2.22	€24.04
2009	2.17	€14.29

Yes, trading turnover was down 40.5% whilst trading volumes remained fairly constant. So, in other words, something else had an impact. What could that be I wonder? From the *Wall Street Journal*:

> "Chi-X Europe, one of the new breed of alternative trading platforms, became the second largest European equities market by value traded in January, leapfrogging incumbent exchanges including the London Stock Exchange (LSE.LN) and Deutsche Bourse (DB1.XE) for the first time. Trading levels for European equities on the electronic order book of the London-based platform, known as a multilateral trading facility, were valued at EUR109 billion ($147 billion) during January, according to figures released today by the Federation of European Securities Exchanges."

Chi-X exploits LSE's weaknesses further (2009)

There's plenty of innovation in banking right now, from investment through commercial to retail banking. And it's not just amongst the big banks, the thriving banks and the growing banks but amongst the struggling banks, the tarnished banks and the zombie banks too. For example, Citi is spending a billion dollars on new payments technologies this year, and there's plenty of innovation in their transactions services business.

But some innovators create new business models at the expense of the incumbents – that's the way it's supposed to be, isn't it?

This is no better illustrated than by the announcement of the London Stock Exchange (LSE) which has faced continuing difficulties, as shown by their 37% drop in profits when the FTSE almost doubled in value during the same period.

This is a strong indication of how innovators are disrupting, such as BATS Europe. But the key innovator with first mover advantage is Chi-X, who launched over two years ago.

Announcing their results for the period between April 1 and September 30, the LSE let it be known that the total number of trades in UK shares dealt on the exchange dropped 17% to 78.4 million, with the value of the shares traded falling 46% to £580 billion.

This is during a period when, between March and August, investors have seen the biggest rally in shares in half a century with the value of British shares up from £454 billion to £1.44 trillion.

This is why Xavier Rolet has cut prices and continues to do so (doesn't work), has shrunk the LSE's workforce by 11% (let's shrink our way out of this), thrown out their TradElect flagship system (which just doesn't work) and is in talks to buy Turquoise (which is also struggling thanks to the Chi-X onslaught).

And how big is that onslaught? Let's put it this way, it now has such a large share of trading in most European exchanges that it is now the third largest trading platform for equities trading, just behind the Deutsche Bourse and Euronext, and bigger than Spain's national stock exchange and the Swiss bourse. It has managed to take a quarter of the trading in the FTSE 100 from the LSE, and this looks likely to increase, especially if LSE's outages continue.

So what does Chi-X go and do? They only announce the next day that they intend to hire Alasdair Haynes, the hotly tipped contender to have taken the job that Xavier Rolet took earlier this year and also back in 2001. In other words, the man who should have been CEO of the LSE is now the CEO of its likely slayer and successor, Chi-X.

Funny how the world turns, isn't it?

It is easy to criticise and hard to strategise – so what would I do if I were heading the LSE?

I would change the battleground and create a new market territory for the LSE outside the razor-thin margins of trading the most liquid stocks. Focus upon creating new markets or generate a new platform offering razor-thin margin trading in other stocks or instruments. The trouble with this strategy is that with 75% of their business tied to the most liquid stocks today, it is too hard to consider as an acceptable approach. It is too radical. The thing is, that all the radical things the LSE has tried so far have failed, and are likely to continue in this fashion unless they do something radical.

Meanwhile, the 75% liquidity isn't going to disappear overnight so keep that fat margin to fund the next generation of thin margin, and broaden and deepen the platforms.

They may well be doing this, with the implementation of MillenniumIT and acquisition of Turquoise, except that both appear to be second choice solutions to compete with Chi-X rather than first choice solutions to create a new battleground.

Roll on the next six months ...

Note: BATS Europe are also doing OK, with Bloomberg reporting that they "aim to do between 8 percent and 10 percent by the end of the next year, doubling our market share in 2010" according to CEO Mark Hemsley. "We have a lot of new firms coming over and we're benefiting from the increasing sophistication of the trading systems of the big brokers we signed up in the first wave."

"Over the past five days, BATS Europe accounted for about 8 percent of UK FTSE 100 trading, 4 percent of France's CAC 40 and 3.3 percent of Germany's DAX on average, according to data from BATS. London-based Chi-X Europe drew about 25 percent, 17 percent and 19 percent, respectively."

Note: Wall Street Journal headline: "MTFs Capture 54% of Europe's Dark Markets"

"A trio of alternative trading systems has seized more than half of Europe's 'dark' equities market from broker-run rivals in just six months.

"Chi-X Europe, Turquoise and BATS Europe together handled 54% of all trades executed by public dark pools in the month to November 19, according to Thomson Reuters. None of the multilateral trading facilities operated a dark pool before May.

"Meanwhile, three established dark pools, Liquidnet Europe, ITG Posit and Nyfix Euro Millennium, saw their share of the market shrink to 39% in November from 98% in May, Thomson Reuters said. ITG launched Posit in 1998, while Liquidnet Europe went live in 2002 and Euro Millennium has been operating for 18 months."

Money for nothing, and my ticks for free (2008)

With BATS Europe saying that it will take 15% to 20% of the FTSE100 trading away from the LSE and other players by the end of 2009, I had a look at their American track record.

Launched in January 2006, BATS achieved an average market share over 10.1% of all American equities trading volumes last month, processing over 1.1 billion shares daily. That's not bad after two and a half years, although still a little ways to go to catch up with the NYSE, who process almost five billion shares daily (4.97), and NASDAQ's near three billion (2.9).

BATS' mission is to shake up a market "where innovation and technology leadership were at risk due to over consolidation in the ECN and exchange industry". In other words, with so much consolidation and liquidity for cash equities trading focused only on the NYSE and NASDAQ, the opportunity had opened up for other players. They've also gained approval to become a proper exchange from the SEC, so BATS has grown up.

Why has BATS become such a force in the US markets? In many ways for the same reasons as Chi-X in Europe: low latency, low prices, low costs guaranteed. BATS made this clear recently, issuing some statistics which showed order processing speeds of between 400 and 500 microseconds per order, with 80% of orders acknowledged within 400 microseconds. A microsecond is one-millionth of a second, so that's 0.0004 seconds! In these days of best execution integrated with algo trading systems, it has become the place to go.

But there's one other aspect that is interesting about BATS: it's for the retail investor, as well as the broker dealer. This year, for example, they have extended their market data feeds into free real-time feeds for AOL and Yahoo! Finance users. In recognition of this move, NASDAQ OMX now delivers free real-time market data to Google, the Wall Street Journal, CNBC and Xignite.

Real-time market data for free on public websites for millions of consumers at home to access. No delay. No fees. No hassle.

I like it ... by the way, how much do we charge for real-time market data in the EU?

Well, Chi-X place all that info on their website:

Trading venue fee for Level 2 data	**License fee (per annum)**	**Per workstation per annum**
Chi-X	£0	£0
Euronext	€36,750	€696
Deutsche Bourse Xetra	€32,400	€816
London Stock Exchange	£44,000	£1,260

How nice of them, and is it any wonder that Chi-X has taken 4% of all European market data volumes over the last six months.

We live in interesting times.

The battering of the London Stock Exchange (2008)

I've been watching MiFID's progress in the background over recent months. I say, in the background, because there's been so much stuff going on in the stock markets after Lehman Brothers that it was not something I felt made the frontground.

Until now. The reason to bring it up now is that it's a year since its implementation, and the London Stock Exchange (LSE) hit the news this week ... and it's bad news, much of it related to the implications of MiFID.

The first part of the bad news is that they need to conserve cash and therefore cancelled their £500 million share buyback scheme. The result was the share price dropped 10% yesterday, closing at just under £5.20p, well below the £12.43p offered by NASDAQ in 2006.

That drop is far higher than other major European Exchanges, such as Euronext and Deutsche Bourse, because the LSE is suffering the bulk of that attack from the new MTFs (Multilateral Trading Facilities) and lacks the alternative systems, such as the Eurex Derivatives of the Deutsche Bourse, to fight back through diversification. Sure, they have a derivatives subsidiary, but it's nowhere near as successful as Eurex.

This leads on to the other bad news from the MTFs: Turquoise and Chi-X.

Turquoise claims that they are taking 5% of the value of trading on LSE's most liquid stocks, whilst Chi-X claims to have achieved an almost 30% market ratio of the trading of the FTSE100 in recent times.

And today is the day that BATS Trading sets off, so it's all pretty gloomy on the equities trading front. That's why trading revenue is down 1.25% and trading value down 2%.

Part of the reason for such loss is that the new MTFs offer 'dark pool' trading facilities, where orders and bids can be placed on exchange without visibility until the order or bid is filled. LSE obviously will compete in this space, and announced the launch of their own dark pool, Baikal, earlier this year.

Baikal would be a joint venture with Lehman Brothers. Whoops. Yes, you guessed it, LSE has to find a new partner for this now and announced that Baikal would be pushed back a quarter to the fall of 2009 before it would see the light of day.

And it's not just losing your most liquid stock trading to new competition that's bugging them, but also losing the profitable business that was known as trade reporting to MarkitBOAT.

This should mean that profitability is hit, but instead the Exchange announced a 30% increase in pre-tax profits, to £127 million for the six months to end of September! Oh well, looking under the numbers, part of this profit came from the merger of Boursa Italiana, and operating profit was up only 5 percent.

As discussed in September, their CEO, Dame Clara Furse, now looks to be on her way out after seven years at the helm. Dame Clara has been a good leader through the predatory times when the LSE was being sought for acquisition by NASDAQ and others. However, you need an aggressive leader who can fight off new competition rather than predators, and that's what the LSE will try to achieve in light of the new landscape of the post-MiFID markets.

All in all, the LSE faces its most challenging time ever, as do the other exchanges. I'm not letting NYSE Euronext and Deutsche Bourse off the hook, just because they are big and diversified. The difference is that they are better positioned to survive the new threats we see after MiFID, due to their diversity and global platforms, than the LSE.

All in all, I just hope it does not mean we talk about London's Old Stock Exchange (LOSE) in the future.

MiFID's new MTFs start to bite (2008)

(...)

In this post-MiFID world, I've been hearing lots of interesting things over the last week about exchanges.

This was particularly in light of a workshop on MiFID I ran for a range of banks, clearers and exchanges looking at the impact of initiatives such as Chi-X, MarkitBOAT, BATS, PLUS Markets and others that are coming downstream, such as Turquoise, Equiduct and Smartpools.

(...)

We then had a meeting of the Financial Services Club with Simon Brickles, Chief Executive of PLUS Markets Group.

PLUS is a new stock exchange in London that gained Recognised Investment Exchange (RIE) status in July 2007. The new trading platform, launched in November 2007, trades over 7,500 stocks primarily in London listed shares, AIM dual-traded stocks, European liquid shares and the over 220 PLUS-quoted stocks (they gained 60 new stock listings in 2007, and a further 19 this year-to-date).

The main focus of PLUS is on small to mid-caps, competing with LSE's smaller exchange, the Alternative Investment Market (AIM), where Simon used to be at the helm. PLUS claim that on 22nd January 2008, they took 53% of all retail equity trading in UK stocks whilst the LSE only processed 47%.

Meanwhile, MarkitBOAT has taken a large chunk of LSE's trade publication revenues, and is now bigger for turnover of trading in European stocks than the LSE.

All in all, for UK equities, LSE has moved from 69.73% of the turnover of shares in November 2007, when MiFID launched, to 61.63% in April 2008; and from 18.35% of all European shares trading by turnover down to 11.79% in April, according to Reuters.

If I were a traditional Bourse therefore, I would be worried. But not if I am the Deutsche Bourse, apparently. Frank Gerstenschläger, an Executive Board member of the Bourse, told the exchange's annual meeting in Frankfurt: "I'm optimistic that liquidity won't transfer to other platforms. There won't be an impact on the company's profitability resulting from new platforms."

I guess LSE and everyone else thought the same as you, Frank, but you might want to smell the coffee.

Are stock exchanges fungible? (2008)

(...)

Are stock exchanges are really fungible? Fungibility is a word I hate, but it is used extensively in the capital markets to identity something that can be traded in a variety of forms.

According to my banking dictionary, fungible applies to any "financial instrument equivalent in value to another, and easily exchanged or substituted". For example gold is fungible. Gold can be exchanged as rings, necklaces, bracelets, nuggets, dust and more. But at the end of the day, gold is gold and has a net value per ounce. It is the different forms that have an equivalent value to each other, but are easily exchanged and substituted in different forms of delivery.

So, in the words of the financial markets, I ask are exchanges fungible? They can be easily substituted for different venues and there is little to keep you in one venue, so why not change?

This is the proposal of all of these new exchanges and execution venues. They are vying for investors and brokers to switch allegiance from their existing preferred venues to the new upstarts. Chi-X for example, claims to be able to do this through speed – processing times of two milliseconds – and price, with the spread reduces to single digits compared to traditional exchanges which have anything up to 20 basis points in the spread.

Price and speed are important, and so Chi-X as a first move is gaining traction. But how many of these execution venues do we need and they cannot all gain business competing on price and speed, as Chi-X are in that space, so what are they going to compete on?

This is a question raised at last week's Derivatives Conference run by FOWeek in London. The question arose because many believed that Turquoise and BOAT were purely cynical ploys from banks to shake up traditional exchanges into lowering fees and spreads. If this is the case, then it has worked, so some ask now whether it is worth launching new exchanges. In particular, the question was being raised about Rainbow and ELX.

ELX, formerly known as Four Seasons, is launching a futures product for the Eurodollar that will compete with the CME Group. The ELX project is owned by a range of financial institutions, including Bank of America, Barclays Capital, Citadel, Citigroup, Credit Suisse, Deutsche Bank Securities, E-Speed, Getco, JPMorgan, Merrill Lynch, Peak6, and Royal Bank of Scotland. Others are expected to join this list including Goldman Sachs, so it should do well you would think. But is it needed?

Similarly, Project Rainbow has been set up to challenge LIFFE, the London Futures Exchange, with backing from Barclays, Deutsche Bank, Goldman Sachs, JPMorgan, MF Global, NewEdge and UBS. It is challenged with gaining a clearing capability, after talks fell through with LCH.Clearnet, but it looks like it is still moving along.

Overall, all of this sounds great in principle, but there are real questions as to how much the market can sustain in terms of trading. Sure, MiFID was meant to create this sort of turmoil and change, but the real question is, where is the end game?

If you ask me, it's liquidity. In this case, gaining market volume of trading and earning your spurs. I know that is obvious but, traditionally, no new market entrant has shifted significant liquidity away from the dominant players. In addition, if any of them do, then the dominant incumbent has simply acquired the upstart or replicated and undercut their service. That is why LSE, NYSE Euronext, NASDAQ, CME, Deutsche Bourse/Eurex have survived so well, so far.

Maybe all of this sabre-rattling in the markets is fun to watch, but I therefore do wonder whether we will see any radical market restructuring away from the incumbents, or whether this is just an evolution of existing business.

Chapter 6 Clearing and settlement

The
Complete
Banker

Introduction

Clearing and settlement is often referred to as the plumbing of the banking industry. For investment banks, capital markets and global trading, an efficient system to clear funds and settle trading is critical to an efficient market. But it is inefficient right now. In Europe and Asia in particular, due to tax laws and barriers to access, most clearing is on a national level, with few regional capabilities. This is bad, as it inhibits global trade, but it's good because it keeps business domestic. Banks are changing the game here, but it's very slow and not very sure, especially as so much is under national government company and fiscal laws. Until it is resolved, the idea of a global trading market will never be realised.

Why is clearing so complex? (2009)

There's been much discussion recently about the issues of clearing and settlement in Europe. You would think if it was clearing, it should be clear ... but it's a real mess of complexity and confusion, if we're honest.

In Europe, part of the issue comes down to the European Commission focusing upon this area after MiFID rather than before. MiFID, you see, focused upon pre-trade equities investments in Europe. The aim was to get rid of the national exchange focused schemes, known as concentration rules, which meant that you had to invest on the national exchange of the country where the stock was listed.

The Commission wanted this to be open to new pan-European services but it has failed because pre-trade is only half the equation. Without post-trade clearing being addressed, where the trades are settled and paid, you cannot have an open and seamless market.

Therefore, MiFID led to a whole raft of issues as the explosion of new MTFs – exchanges like Chi-X, Burgundy, Turquoise, NASDAQ OMX and Equiduct – spawned a range of new and competing clearing systems, including SIX x-clear, EuroCCP and the EMCF.

MiFID also saw a dramatic rise in the use of dark pools, where trading blocks of orders is hidden from public view. These dark pools include systems run by the exchanges such as Baikal (London Stock Exchange) and Smartpool (Euronext), along with privately owned dark pools of market makers such as Goldman Sachs (SIGMA X) and UBS (Price Improvement Network), as well as those of the new MTF exchanges.

Then you have the new Electronic Liquidity Providers, such as GETCO, who create even more off exchange auto trading.

Result? A mass of new trading venues and systems leading to the fragmentation of pricing and risk, and potentially making the markets more risk oriented due to the competitive nature of the brokers, exchanges and clearers involved.

This risk issue is demonstrated by the arguments EuroCCP are making over risk management, where their CEO has asked for an agreed convention in this space. Equally, reports of Goldman Sachs market manipulating doesn't help.

These are the laws of unintended consequences, and they are all putting pressure upon creating a MiFID 2 to answer key questions around a consolidated pricing system, transparency in dark pools, the real definition of 'best execution' and how to create pan-European clearing systems that are truly comparable.

These are all questions challenging the Committee of European Securities Regulators (CESR), soon to become the European Securities Authority.

A core question in all of this relates to clearing and settlement. Clearing and settlement was just plain missed when the European Commission began its lawmaking processes; and the problem with clearing and settlement is that traditional exchanges, protected by their concentration rules before MiFID, have raised barriers to pan-European trading due to the nature of their silo structures, where the clearing systems are integrated with the national exchanges.

Where the clearing and settlement systems are exchange owned and operated, the incumbents can lock-in and force buyers to trade and clear through the exchange, as they can't get access to go anywhere else.

Some of these things are changing, but the change is so slow that, by comparison, watching paint dry or grass grow or snails race is invigorating.

Now, thanks to the frustration of the new players, especially EuroCCP (owned by America's DTCC) and EMCF (operated by Fortis and changing to new owners post the crash of Fortis), things may change.

These new players believe they can offer clearing at a fraction of the cost of the vertically integrated groups, but they are unable to access the markets. This is due to the barriers to trade and interoperability. In fact, it is pretty much impossible to even compare products and services across these markets that lock them out.

Change we can believe in

Where is the change coming from?

Well, it began back in 2001 with the Giovannini Committee chaired by Alberto Giovannini. This group analysed the issues to clearing and settlement across Europe and released a report in 2003 outlining 15 barriers to trade. Most of these are industry related – transparency and access issues – although the most important barriers relate to government policies as they focus upon taxation and company law.

In 2003, the Giovannini report reckoned we could get rid of these barriers by 2006. Guess what? Didn't happen.

Therefore, in order to try to resolve such issues, the European Commission implemented a Code of Conduct for Clearing and Settlement in 2006. The Code of Conduct came into force in January 2008 and has had sign-up from most clearers across Europe to resolve the issues of interoperability, whilst bringing in pricing transparency and unbundled products such that they could be more comparable.

It hasn't worked, however. The Code of Conduct has reduced some barriers, but not much. You still cannot compare products between CCPs across markets. You therefore still cannot get a clear pricing structure or comparison. And, no matter how hard you try, you still cannot see true interoperability across markets.

If you could, you wouldn't need the creation of Trade2Clear, a working group comprising most of the new clearing systems recently announced.

In fact, you have three clear groups of clearers: the challengers, the incumbents and the gorilla.

The challengers are in the Trade2Clear camp which are the exchanges of Chi-X Europe, London Stock Exchange, Turquoise, Burgundy, NASDAQ OMX Europe and Equiduct; along with their clearers – LCH.Clearnet, SIX x-clear, EMCF, Monte Titoli and EuroCCP.

Then there is a second group of incumbents led by Clearstream, which has created a thing called the Linkup Markets alliance. The Linkup Markets crowd covers key securities depositories from Clearstream Banking AG Frankfurt in Germany through CSE, Cyprus; the Hellenic Exchanges S.A., Greece; IBERCLEAR of Spain; Oesterreichische Kontrollbank AG from Austria; SIX SIS

AG of Switzerland (those Swiss get everywhere don't they?); and VP Securities, Denmark along with VPS of Norway.

The final bit is the single platform developments of Euroclear, which covers the rest of Europe. Their focus is to create a massive single platform for European clearing.

These three camps are vying for supremacy and standards, access and transparency, and clear pricing with comparability.

But it's not happening.

More change to come

This discussion thus far does not even mention the impact of other new things, such as TARGET2 for Securities (T2S), the ECB's settlement service that combines collateral management (CCBM2) with settlement services.

T2S aims to get rid of most national Securities Settlement Systems and, as one person commented last week, "what incentive is there to get rid of 40% of your reason for existence?" This is in reference to the fact that most national Central Securities Depositories (CSDs) have half their business processing settlements ... and that's the half they're now being forced to give up if it transitions to T2S.

Nor does it mention the latest craze to develop a single repository – not depository – for OTC derivatives, along with clearing and other requirements in this market.

Nor the latest announcements which build upon the Code of Conduct and bring together the cumulative work of the European System of Central Banks (ESCB) and the Committee of European Securities Regulators (CESR). These were published in a report: "Recommendations for securities settlement systems and central counterparties in the European Union" in June.

These recommendations are based upon an eight-year gestation period (that's longer than it takes to give birth to a nation!) from the draft recommendations for securities settlement systems that were proposed in November 2001; and the recommendations for CCPs issued by the Committee on Payment and Settlement Systems (CPSS) and the Technical Committee of the International Organization of Securities Commissions (CPSS-IOSCO) back in November 2004 .

What was I saying about paint drying being more exciting?

Nor does it mention the relationship between central clearing at a national versus regional versus global level. Bearing in mind that we are talking these days about global markets requiring global regulations and regulators, regional operations for such global markets may not make so much sense anymore?

Nevertheless, first things first, let's get the EU act together and, to do this, it means that there is now a very strong justification for a dictate to get this thing done.

A dictate means a Directive.

A Clearing and Settlement Directive

The industry doesn't want this because they don't like prescriptive regulation. Therefore, the industry will say the Code of Conduct works and continue to try to pretend this is gaining traction.

The European Commission doesn't want this, because it means encroaching on member state's laws for tax and fiscal reporting. Half the activities of securities depositories for example are involved in corporate actions, the payments of dividend and the calculation of taxes. The Commission doesn't want to get into a bun-fight with national governments to attack this stuff.

But you know what? Without getting involved, this space will just languish as a mess of clearing. And that's the last thing we want in light of the recent crisis, so guess what? A Clearing and Settlement Directive for Europe is on its way. Draft legislation for consultative purposes is probably going to be published within a year or so, and then transposition in 2012. This is pure supposition on my part, but I just don't see any other way around this.

A mess of clearing ... (2009)

This week has been spent in a debate about clearing and settlement systems, and the most interesting dialogue has been about the US versus EU approaches.

The American system exists with a few core clearing systems based around the major exchanges – the Intercontinental and the Chicago Mercantile – along with the DTCC, which provides clearing for the US NYSE and NASDAQ markets and more.

In Europe, we have CSDs (Central Securities Depositories) and CCPs (Central Counterparty Clearing systems) for almost every country, in some cases more than one per country.

This creates issues of risk fragmentation, but also the opportunity for some to lock customers into their structures by being vertically integrated with the stock exchanges. Equally, it is virtually impossible to compare products and services of these integrated clearing systems, because they bundle everything into packages of products that make them incomparable with any others.

The challenge is illustrated by the range and specialities of clearers.

For example, there are several new clearing operations across Europe, including SIX x-clear, EMCF and EuroCCP; as well as others who are trying to shake things up such as Monte Titoli and LCH.Clearnet. There are derivative product clearers, such as Eurex Clearing (Deutsche Bourse) and LIFFE Clearing (NYSE Euronext); as well as many country based operations from CCP (Austria) to CC&G (Italy), from KDPW (Poland) to KELER (Hungary) and more.

We now are trying to regulate OTC markets and already believe we need to create more infrastructure for Europe, with our own data repository and clearing system.

Great. All in all, this means we just have too many CCPs across Europe, and there is a strong argument that there should be just one CCP. This is the same argument as there was in SEPA for a PEACH, but stronger as securities clearing creates systemic risks if it is fragmented. Furthermore if CCPs compete, as this lot definitely are, it seems to mean that they take their eye off the ball in terms of managing counterparty credit risk.

The issue is safety versus competitiveness, risk management versus cost and transparency versus margin. This needs to be sorted out, and the European Commission will do something about this. The question is how long it will take them to get there.

Clearing is becoming clearer ... (2009)

An interesting announcement on clarifying the standards came out today.

The Committee on Payment and Settlement Systems (CPSS) and the Technical Committee of the International Organization of Securities Commissions (IOSCO) have set up a working group to review the application of the 2004 CPSS-IOSCO Recommendations for Central Counterparties to clearing arrangements for over-the-counter (OTC) derivatives. The recommendations, which were developed by the CPSS and the IOSCO Technical Committee, set out standards for risk management of a central counterparty.

In recent years, there have been coordinated efforts by the public and private sector to improve bilateral clearing and settlement arrangements for OTC derivatives transactions. More recently, several existing, newly established, and proposed central counterparties (CCPs) have sought to provide central clearing and settlement services for OTC credit default swap (CDS) transactions, interest rate swaps, and other asset classes of OTC derivatives.

The CPSS and IOSCO believe that the expansion of centralized clearing and settlement is a positive development because, if well designed, CCPs can reduce systemic risk in financial markets. Accordingly, the relevant authorities for CCPs for OTC derivatives seek to ensure that each CCP meets the risk management standards set forth in the recommendations. However, applying the recommendations in practice can involve a significant degree of interpretation and judgment.

To promote consistent interpretation, understanding and application of the recommendations across CCPs for OTC derivatives, the working group has been formed to discuss key issues that can arise when CCPs, including the new CDS CCPs, provide central clearing services for OTC derivatives. Where necessary, the working group will propose guidance on how CCPs for OTC derivatives may meet the standards set out by the recommendations and will identify any areas in which the recommendations might be strengthened or expanded to better address risks associated with the central clearing of OTC derivatives.

Participants in the working group include representatives of the central banks that are members of the CPSS, representatives of the securities regulators that are members of the IOSCO Technical Committee, and representatives of the International Monetary Fund and the World Bank.

The working group will coordinate with other regulatory authorities and communicate with the industry, as appropriate, as the work moves forward.

By way of background, the CPSS is a forum for central banks to monitor and analyse developments in payment and settlement arrangements as well as in cross-border and multicurrency settlement schemes.

IOSCO is the international policy forum for securities regulators. The organisation's membership regulates more than 95% of the world's securities markets in over 100 jurisdictions, and its membership is steadily growing.

The Technical Committee is a specialised working group established by IOSCO's Executive Committee, and is made up of 18 agencies that regulate some of the world's larger, more developed and internationalised markets. Its objective is to review major regulatory issues related to international securities and futures transactions and to coordinate practical responses to these concerns.

The members of the Technical Committee come from Australia, Brazil, China, France, Germany, Hong Kong SAR, India, Italy, Japan, Mexico, the Netherlands, Ontario, Quebec, Spain, Switzerland, the UK and the US.

Jamie Dimon: a CCP for OTC is bad (2009)

JP Morgan's Jamie Dimon has called for a rethink of the central clearing system for OTC derivatives that everyone wants to see in play.

The clearing and settlement area is the plumbing of financial service, where all risks of sellers or buyers defaulting are managed by the clearer acting as the buyer to the seller and the seller to the buyer. By having a Central CounterParty (CCP) for clearing, the market has confidence.

Unfortunately, in the case of OTC derivative, such as credit default swaps (CDS), there was no CCP. As a result, there was panic and fear after the collapse of Lehmans as every $1 billion in CDS contracts outstanding could lead to losses of between $18 to $22 billion for all the counterparties involved. The fear was also that the clearing systems might not cope, but they managed nicely.

The DTCC for example, announced that they had sorted out half a trillion dollars worth of Lehman contracts within six weeks of the collapse. In reality, this meant the DTCC sorts out all of the exposures related to the investment bank and its counterparties, netting down positions, becoming the buyer to every seller and the seller to every buyer.

After this debacle, everyone has since been talking about creating a CCP for these products, as one did not exist for OTC derivatives, and there are four groups scurrying around to do this:

- CME Group and Citadel;
- Eurex Clearing, part of Deutsche Bourse;
- IntercontinentalExchange (ICE) with The Clearing Corporation; and
- NYSE Euronext and LCH.Clearnet, Europe's largest clearing systems.

According to the BBC's Robert Peston, however, Jamie Dimon decided to pour doubt over the creation of the CCP for OTC. Mr. Peston reports that Jamie Dimon told the World Economic Forum's governors' meeting not to put too much faith in the creation of a central clearing system, because it would mean banks would think less about who they were buying, selling, lending and investing to and with. He claimed that the current crisis was caused by banks not knowing their customers and that the more banks are protected and insured against losses on lending, the more they will lend irresponsibly.

Maybe Mr. Dimon has this view as his bank is one of the largest traders in OTC derivatives, with $87 trillion in derivatives and $10 trillion in CDS?

A borderless, neutral single market for securities across Europe (2008)

The phrase "a borderless, neutral single market for securities across Europe" is one that appears regularly throughout all communications on settlement services from the European Central Bank (ECB) and European Commission.

In fact, it appeared a lot last Friday, when the ECB released two key documents: the TARGET2 for Securities (T2S) User Requirements and Collateral Central Bank Management (CCBM2) User Requirements.

The importance of these two announcements, in the context of clearing and settlement, cannot be stressed enough as the combination of T2S and CCBM2 are intended to create this "borderless, neutral single market for securities across Europe" by creating a single infrastructure for counterparty liquidity and collateralisation.

According to the ECB, T2S aims to:

- Reduce all settlement costs by avoiding duplicative investment in a mature product and cut "cross border" costs from the outset;
- Promote competition by unbundling settlement from custody, issuer servicing, provision of cash for settlement and collateral management services across a single Europe-wide pool of securities; and
- Drive harmonisation to make Europe a better place to invest and trade as part of the Lisbon agenda and Financial Services Action Plan.

Whilst CCBM2 aims to cover the collateralised credit provision for the NCBs of the Eurosystem by:

- Providing collateral handling functionalities;
- Handling an important part of the monetary policy implementation; and
- Providing intra-day credit in central bank money to allow TARGET2 to run smoothly.

T2S will be developed and operated by Deutsche Bundesbank, the Banco de España, the Banque de France and the Banca d'Italia; whilst CCBM2 will be developed and operated by the

Nationale Bank van België and De Nederlandsche Bank. This is true co-operation across Europe, in other words.

T2S now has the green light for launch, with both systems expected to be in operation by 2013 at the latest. That may seem a long way away, but as others have pointed out, the various connections, interconnections, pipes and plumbing that goes around all this will take a long time to change and upgrade. Therefore, T2S has a:

- Specification phase now through 2009;
- Development phase through 2011; and
- Migration and testing through 2013,

at which point the production systems go live.

The outline of how these two systems will work in practice is charted below:

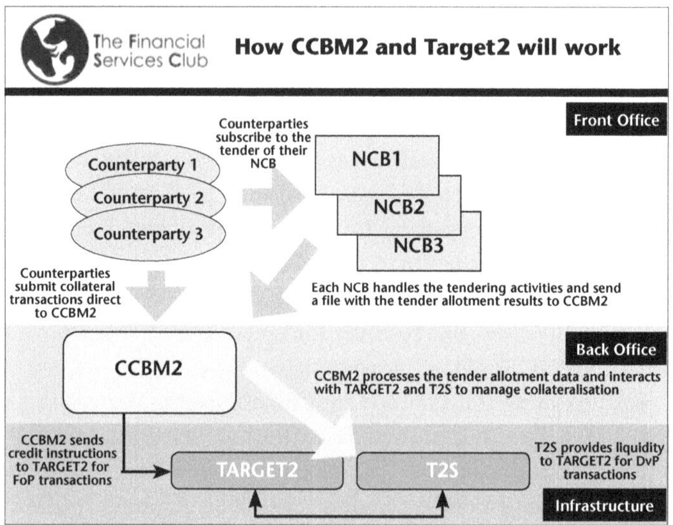

What this shows is that the whole process of counterparty tendering and collateralisation through to settlement, becomes a single platform model through interoperability between T2S and CCBM2. Straight-through processing of euro settlement services.

For T2S specifically, and its linkages to CSDs and NCBs, the process flow is outlined as:

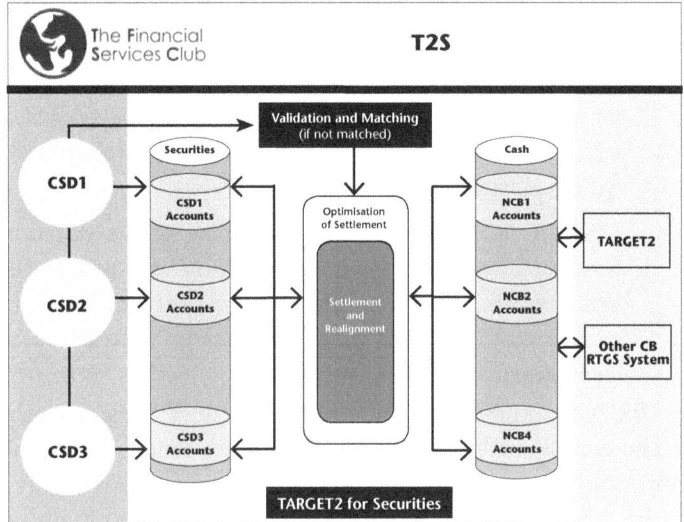

As can be seen, this does become a 'cloud computing' style capability for CSDs, NCBs and counterparties to enable straight through euro settlement services. As a result, the ECB believes an integrated securities settlement infrastructure in the euro zone will cut settlement costs by up to 90%.

You can read exactly what this means to CSDs and NCBs in the newsletter released by the ECB on Wednesday. Here are a few choice words from ECB Board Member, Gertrude Tumpel-Gugerell:

> "Cross-border settlement within Europe in central bank money should become at least as secure, efficient and cheap as settlement in the best domestic market is today."

> "The Eurosystem will play the roles of catalyst and service provider, but it will be the market itself that creates a borderless, neutral single market for securities across Europe ... By creating a single, neutral pool of European assets, T2S will stimulate competition among service providers. Higher market volumes will be an incentive for intermediaries to improve their economies of scale and to develop new offers for the users' benefit. More liquidity will also be available, with substantial gains for investors and for capital users. T2S will foster harmonisation."

> "There is a risk of a possible widening of the distance between the euro area and the rest of the EU. We are pleased that several European countries – even outside the EU – have committed to T2S, and we will continue to welcome such commitments."

The bottom line is that the free movement of funds through a "borderless, neutral single market for securities" has many implications.

From SWIFT's viewpoint, FIN messaging, ISO20022, working to enable easy access and interoperability is all a core part of this activity.

Equally, there's been lots of dialogue between SWIFT, the ECB, the CSDs and the NCBs about whether T2S is really needed. What are the real implications of T2S?

In the medium term, T2S and CCBM2 imply redundancy of national systems within the Eurozone, although whether NCBs will remove such systems is one question. More importantly, it dictates that CSDs will need to focus outside of settlement services, which will become commoditised. This means focus upon corporate actions, repo, custody and other value-added services.

This is why you see the ICSDs in particular responding with new initiatives, such as the Single Platform from Euroclear. This will bring all of Euroclear's CSD systems onto a single service that will "harmonise the various practices for settlement, custody, payments, reference data and tax". This, alongside Clearstream's Linked Up Markets leadership, is changing the landscape of European settlement services to achieve the Eurocrat's aspirations.

So then, I ask, why a Clearing and Settlement Directive?

Sure, the Code of Conduct and more is not working as hoped but T2S, CCBM2, Linked Up Markets, Euroclear's Single Platform, EuroCCP and EMCF and others are all clamouring to change things. Is a Directive really needed?

What's the solution for clearing and settlement? (2008)

The International Central Securities Depositories (ICSDs) of Euroclear and Clearstream are very competitive with and against each other and there are many other services that CSDs offer other than just settlement. The Linked Up Markets group and other activities are starting to change the landscape of these end game post-trade activities but, right now, the more interesting area for me is clearing.

This is because we have two significant new clearing facilities in Europe: the EuroCCP from the DTCC and the European Multilateral Clearing Facility (EMCF) from Fortis. This is not to overlook x-Clear from SIS in Switzerland or other movers and shakers, but EuroCCP and EMCF are, for me, indicating the future trends in clearing and settlement.

Why? Because they are aligned with the post-MiFID shake-out we are seeing in the pre-trade environment.

The fact is that MiFID has changed the European game, with the launch of many new equities trading facilities such as Turquoise, Plusmarkets, Chi-X, Equiduct, NASDAQ OMX, BATS Trading, NYFIX Millenium and Equiduct.

Then there are the knock-on effects in data reporting, derivatives and other markets, such as Boat and Rainbow. Then there's the dark pools arising, with SWX launching Swiss Block in August, Euronext launching Smartpool around the same time and the LSE launching Baikal with Lehman early next year.

All of these launches are based upon pushing the boundaries of technology interconnectivity and low latency to maximise the opportunities for generating new liquidity and alpha returns across Europe's deregulated investment markets.

What this also means is that we are starting to see a restructuring of clearing and settlement operations.

The start point is the realignment of markets as these new players create new clearing operations. EMCF are very aggressive in this area, having signed up NASDAQ OMX, Chi-X and BATS Trading. EuroCCP are equally as aggressive, contracting with Turquoise and Smartpool.

In fact, EuroCCP are so aggressive that they issued a study of pricing across Europe's clearing landscape on 1st July to show how cheap they are. Here's what they found:

Country	Exchange	CCP	Average clearing cost/side (€)
Austria	Wiener Börse	CCP.A	0.07
Belgium, France, Netherlands, Portugal	NYSE LCH. Euronext	Clearnet SA	0.23
Denmark, Finland, Sweden + Baltics	NASDAQ OMX	Fortis EMCF	0.14
Germany	Deutsche Bourse	Eurex Clearing AG	0.55
Ireland	Irish Stock Exchange	Eurex Clearing AG	0.32
Italy	Borsa Italiana	CC&G	0.09
Norway	Oslo Børs	Fortis EMCF	0.14
Switzerland	SWX Group	SIS x-clear	0.20
UK	LSE	LCH.Clearnet Ltd	0.19
Pan-Europe	Turquoise	EuroCCP	0.0292

I like the fact that the EuroCCP could calculate their processing costs to four decimal points, rather than rounding it up to two (€0.03). I was also amused that EMCF claim that EuroCCP charge an average €0.06 per side, so they immediately dropped their pricing, introduced on 1st July 2008 as €0.10, to €0.05 from 1st August.

Meanwhile, LCH.Clearnet's pricing has been dropping faster than Gordon Brown's confidence, with multiple reductions ever since these guys and x-clear appeared on the scene. LCH.Clearnet claim that the EuroCCP's charts are not comparing apples with apples (heard that before) and that, on a like-for-like comparison with EuroCCP's figures, they would process for around €0.055 per side.

Whatever. The bottom line is that costs are falling rapidly across Europe's pre- and post- trade landscape.

The combined cost of processing has decreased by 75%, according to Turquoise. Add on to this that you have:

- Much lower latency, with the new exchanges claiming sub-three millisecond order processing, compared to over 200 milliseconds previously;
- Systems built for 21st century technology processes, specifically algorithmics, which is why new liquidity and dark pool processing is arising;
- You have pan-European access through a single provider, rather than local access through a national exchange,

and you can start to see this rippling effect of change.

The change is that no part of financial services is untouched by the Financial Services Action Plan, just as the Commission hoped, because the markets are adapting to take advantage.

The markets, and their buy-side customers, are placing pressure on all providers to pull their socks up and get competitive or they'll walk. After all, why would you stay with a broker-dealer, exchange, clearer or settlement provider who charged you four times as much for a slower service using proprietary 20th century technologies?

What's the problem with clearing and settlement then? (2008)

In the context of clearing and settlement, we have an issue. The issue is one of transparency, access, interoperability and accounting. The European Commission, Alberto Giovannini, the Code of Conduct and the Monitoring Group have all tried to change this, but it is not changing fast enough.

What's the problem? The problem is that:

- You cannot compare apples with apples;
- Clearing and settlement involves many constituencies that are fragmented and protecting their turf;
- Settlement is dictated often by national rules of company law and taxation systems; and
- There's no incentive to change, not even the threat of punitive measures by the European Commission, because CCPs and CSDs have protection from both governmental and historical structures in many instances.

However, things are changing and, to understand this, we need to evaluate the structure we are trying to change.

On the one hand you have the large counterparty and central counterparty clearing operations, the CCPs. The primary operators here are:

- CC&G for Borsa Italiana, Italy;
- CCP.A for Weiner Bourse, Austria ;
- Eurex Clearing AG for Deutsche Bourse, Germany and Ireland ;
- EuroCCP for the new exchange, Turquoise;

- Fortis EMCF for NASDAQ OMX across Denmark, Finland, Sweden and the Baltics, as well as the Oslo Bourse, Norway and the new pan-European exchanges of BATS Trading and Chi-X;
- LCH.Clearnet Ltd for the London Stock Exchange, UK;
- LCH.Clearnet SA for NYSE Euronext across Belgium, France, Netherlands, & Portugal ;
- SIS x-clear for SWX Group, Switzerland .

You can think of these as being big PayPals – they take on the risk of the payer not paying and the seller not selling, during the exchange of monies for securities.

This leads on to, on the other hand, the large Central Securities Depositories, the CSDs:

- Clearstream (Germany);
- Euroclear (Belgium, France and Netherlands) which also owns CREST (UK) and is expanding to Finland and Sweden through the acquisition of NCSD;
- Hellenic Exchanges (Greece);
- IBERCLEAR (Spain);
- Oesterreichische Kontrollbank (Austria);
- SIS SegaInterSettle (Switzerland);
- VP Securities Services (Denmark);
- VPS (Norway).

As can be seen, CSDs can be confusing because half of them are called 'clear', which implies they perform clearing operations, whereas they are actually settlement operations. The difference is that these are actually more like the logistics operators, exchanging the actual securities certificates for payments. In other words, rather than being the PayPal on eBay, they are the banking and postal logistics firms behind this.

Combined, these CSDs deal with trillions of euros of assets each day, particularly the International CSDs. For example, Euroclear's turnover was €561.8 trillion for 2007. Meanwile,

Clearstream has formed the Link Up Markets Group with the six other CSDs. Their aim is to create a seamless capability to settle across Austria, Denmark, Germany, Greece, Norway, Spain and Switzerland, using Clearstream's technology capabilities. These seven CSDs processed 156 million transactions in 2006, representing almost half of all European securities, and have €12 trillion in assets under custody.

So there are some changes coming through that the Commission desires. You do have competition in Europe, thanks to the launch of BATS Trading, Chi-X and Turquoise. These new exchanges are creating new CCPs, such as EuroCCP and EMCF, and the Link Up Markets is a fundamental shift towards consolidated CSD structures. The traditional exchanges are being challenged and their models of business shaken up. That is the desire of the Commission and the raison d'être behind MiFID and the Code of Conduct.

In particular, the aim is to break apart what some have seen as 'monopolistic' practices, whereby traditional operations have been vertically integrated. The London Stock Exchange is cleared through LCH.Clearnet and settled through Crestco/Euroclear. The Deutsche Bourse is cleared through Eurex Clearing and settled through Clearstream. You want to use someone else? Tough.

This is the bit that needs to change if we are to really have a competitive landscape, and maybe that landscape is already being formed. For example, BATS Trading, Chi-X and NASDAQ OMX using Fortis's EMCF is possibly changing the model of European trading, clearing and settlement.

However, some claim that there are still a range of restrictive practices, particularly amongst the consolidating CSDs. For example, CRESTCo expects you to have been clearing in the market for a certain period of time to join them, and then pay annual membership fees and transaction fees amounting to several hundreds of thousands of pounds per year to be a 'member' of CRESTCo. Some would say that the fact that you can only settle trades on the London Stock Exchange through CRESTCo makes this a barrier to entry.

On the other hand, the fact that the changes made thus far have targeted the vertically integrated structure of the exchanges is having some impact. For example, LCH.Clearnet's pricing has significantly reduced in the last few years, down to what they claim today is only 4 pence ($0.08/€0.05) per transaction, which is highly competitive.

Nevertheless, there are other issues the Commission is targeting. For example, there is meant to be an ability to compare apples with apples between CCPs and CSDs, but this is virtually impossible.

You only need to look at the European CSD Association's (ECSDA) response to the Commission's Code of Conduct to see the issue. The ECSDA proposed comparison tables to assist the Code of Conduct. These Comparison Tables for Price Transparency were meant to:

- Translates the Code's requirements on price comparability into an easy and practical tool easing comparability between heterogeneous pieces of information;
- Provide a table that 'maps' the entries of the CSDs' tariff brochures to a set of common service definitions, based on the Commission's definitions for post-trading; and
- Allow users to trace more easily the relevant fee that each CSD charges for a particular service.

The purpose of the table was not to change or harmonise the CSDs' service offerings or tariff structures, however. As a result, each CSD has very different offerings and the table becomes meaningless because you still cannot compare. In response to this activity, the ECB reviewed this work through the Monitoring Group of the Code of Conduct (MOG) and found that:

- Implementation was not always consistent with ECSDA guidelines and glossary;
- The tables are not always being kept up-to-date; and
- There is no single website covering all CSD conversion tables, which makes comparability more complex.

For example, for each category of the conversion table, some CSDs have a wide variety of services. Taking just one area to illustrate this, the ECSDA proposed eight categories of services relating to 'account provision and asset servicing', one of which is called 'asset servicing of dematerialised securities'. In this category, CSDs entered a total of 172 different services, with some having 23 offers whilst others only have seven or eight.

This is why it is hard to compare these capabilities, because every CSD is different.

Between the complexity of breaking apart vertical trading, clearing and settlement chains; gaining some perspective of comparability; eradicating restrictive practices; and clarifying national tax and company laws; you have a real soup of complexity. This is why the Commission has had such a hard time getting the clearing and settlement space to be resolved.

And, even with a Directive, it will take time. A lot more time. Maybe the real solution however, will lie with the markets – the customers – rather than the regulators and legislators.

Clearing – the last barrier to a financially unified Europe? (2008)

This question occurs to me because it's top of mind with Charlie McCreevy, the European Commission and also many of the discussions taking place today in Paris at a tradeshow focused upon investment banking. Buy and sell side firms have gathered to debate algorithmic trading, dark pools of liquidity, multilateral trading facilities (MTFs), smart order routing, the credit crisis, low latency and more.

To set the context, we begin by talking about technology and it amazes me how blasé we have become about technology. For example, the investment banks talk about low latency, but what does it mean in practice?

Well, the new equities exchange Chi-X claim to process a trade in two milliseconds. How fast is two milliseconds? A human blink is meant to take 200 milliseconds – don't ask me who measured that one – and therefore Chi-X processes orders in a hundredth of the time it takes you to blink your eyes.

That's low latency.

We then move on to talk about MiFID, which is now six months old and is meant to radically shake up Europe's investment markets by guaranteeing best execution and trading transparency.

We have a dialogue around what MiFID means in practice and, in practice, it is too early to say. For example, we had lots of discussions about MiFID's benefits and impact, and most people said they have not seen the benefits or the impact ... yet.

However, with Chi-X claiming to process 13% of the FTSE100 equities on a trading day last week and one of the large trading firms telling me that they now place almost half their trading through Chi-X, there has definitely been some impact.

Equally the AITE Group, a research firm, say that the NYSE's market share of equities trading has halved in the last decade thanks to the US equivalent of MTFs: ATS, Alternative Trading Systems. AITE estimates that 25% of all equities are now traded through ATS, rising to 40% in 2011, with firms such as BATS Trading – the US equivalent of Chi-X that is now launching over here – definitely being at the forefront.

This is the likely long-term impact of MiFID on Europe, with a whole range of players claiming they can offer faster, cheaper, better services than traditional exchanges., including

MarkitBOAT, Turquoise, Virt-x (now SWX), Chi-X, Equiduct, NASDAQ/OMX and more. For example OMX, now owned by NASDAQ, claim that transaction costs for trading in Europe are six times higher than in the USA. OMX will launch a EU300 highly liquid exchange service in September, with the expectation that transaction costs will be a fifth of those charged today.

So, MiFID should result in a lot of trading moving away from traditional exchanges towards new MTFs over time.

This sounds good in principle, but if the exchanges are locked into clearing systems that are slower, more expensive, proprietary and uncompetitive, then all the benefits are lost. After all, the control of clearing creates a clear barrier to shifting execution venues.

This has also been discussed before and is now hot, hot, hot on the EU's agenda. Charlie McCreevy has made clear that clearing and settlement must change from the lack of interoperability today, towards free flowing and open markets tomorrow.

Mr. McCreevy makes it clear that member states must implement the Code of Conduct for interoperability between clearing and settlement infrastructures now, and remove the Giovannini barriers. He concludes: "Some market participants have been arguing that eliminating the Giovannini barriers will not suffice to have true competition in the post-trading arena. They claim that further obstacles exist in some Member States. These obstacles either prevent entry from – or create unfair bias against - providers of clearing and settlement from outside that Member State. As I have said on other occasions, if such obstacles exist, the Commission will demand that they be rapidly dismantled."

I think he means business, especially as his speech threatens regulation in the clearing markets if the voluntary application of the Code fails. He is adamant that the fragmentation of clearing systems across Europe must change.

Alternatively, it may not even require regulatory change as market forces may determine the outcome. For example the Euro CCP, the European clearing arm of the USA's Depository Trust & Clearing Corporation (DTCC), will shake up the EU clearing market anyway now that Turquoise – the new exchange for banks, as I think of it – has chosen the Euro CCP as their clearer of choice.

Between regulatory and European enforced change, technology change and new competitive changes, Europe's investment markets have never been more challenging or more interesting.

www.ingramcontent.com/pod-product-compliance
Ingram Content Group UK Ltd.
Pitfield, Milton Keynes, MK11 3LW, UK
UKHW041825200726
13854UKWH00002BA/572